Rainbow Knits
for Kids

CHERYL POTTER

Martingale®
& C O M P A N Y

Dedication

For the original finger-paint kids, my daughters, Jenna and Cheyenne

Acknowledgments

Thanks to all of the people at Martingale & Company for making this project such a pleasurable experience, and especially Karen Soltys for believing in a book featuring hand-painted knits for children. I would also like to thank the many designers who put in tireless hours on individual projects, particularly JoAnne Turcotte of Plymouth Yarn, whose effort went beyond the cause. Lastly, I would like to thank my family for enduring my early-morning absences and the staff at Cherry Tree Hill for helping me assemble the projects. It really was a group effort. Thanks to all!

Cheryl Potter

Rainbow Knits for Kids
© 2005 by Cheryl Potter

Martingale & Company
20205 144th Avenue NE
Woodinville, WA 98072-8478 USA
www.martingale-pub.com

Credits

President: Nancy J. Martin
CEO: Daniel J. Martin
Publisher: Jane Hamada
Editorial Director: Mary V. Green
Managing Editor: Tina Cook
Technical Editor: Karen Costello Soltys
Copy Editor: Liz McGehee
Design Director: Stan Green
Illustrator: Robin Strobel
Cover and Text Designer: Stan Green
Studio Photographer: Brent Kane
Fashion Photographer: John P. Hamel
Fashion Stylist: Susan Huxley

Printed in China
10 09 08 07 06 05   8 7 6 5 4 3 2 1

Mission Statement

Dedicated to providing quality products and service to inspire creativity.

Library of Congress Cataloging-in-Publication Data

Potter, Cheryl.

Rainbow knits for kids / Cheryl Potter.
  p. cm.
  ISBN 1-56477-564-X
  1. Knitting—Patterns. 2. Children's clothing. I. Title.
  TT825.P68 2005
  746.43′20432—dc22

2004020683

Contents

Preface

Y ARN FOR KIDS' wear does not have to be monochromatic acrylic purchased from discount-department stores. In fact, garments knit from hand-painted natural fibers are for everyone, not just grown-ups. In this book, with the help of some talented designers, I've paired the vibrancy of painted yarn made of quality fiber with practical patterns geared for active children. Whimsical and bright colorways that typically might find their way to the needles of only the more adventuresome sock knitters lend themselves perfectly to children's wear. If you have never tried knitting with painted yarns, here's your chance to delight on a small scale!

What I call "kidability" is a big part of this book. Successful children's knitwear must be soft against the skin and easily laundered. At the same time, both kids and parents like bright, easy-to-wear clothes that are not pretentious or fussy. To provide ease both to the knitter and wearer, I have devised a variety of yarns, from washable, preshrunk cottons that take the hand-dyed colors nicely, to Superwash merinos that are buttery soft and machine washable, to new novelties that are fun to knit and fun to wear.

Over the years, I have hand painted yarns for children's clothing that range from the finest cashmeres to the bulkiest cottons. The scarcity of painted designs for kids, paired with yarns milled with children in mind, prompted me to develop some patterns for my hand-dye company, Cherry Tree Hill. Even so, I noticed there were no pattern books. I could not understand why.

When I asked knitwear designers, some said that painted yarns were too difficult to care for. Others said painted yarns were too expensive. Still others pointed out that painted yarns can be a challenge to knit. But when I went to trade shows, I listened to knitters, and what I heard was the opposite: knitters were hungry for a book devoted to knitting hand paints for children.

Knitting for kids does not have to be expensive, nor must hand-painted garments be relegated to the cedar chest as precious family heirlooms. In fact, many children's sweaters, vests, hats, and socks require so little yarn that these small projects can be knit very quickly and at a reasonable price. I think you will find that you can complete the garments in this book with much less expense and much more quickly than grown-up patterns and that you'll want to make many of the different garments and accessories for the little folks in your life.

Color combinations tend to be bolder and more whimsical for children, and what better way to explore the different colorways afforded by hand-painted yarn than to use them for children's knitwear? Hand-painted yarns will lend each garment a playful appeal to you, the knitter, as the colors merge and diverge row by row. These colorful patterns, in turn, delight the wearers.

Knitters deserve the reward of working with quality fibers and vibrant colors as they carve hours from their busy schedules to knit for children. As a dyer and designer, it is my pleasure to honor kids' knits with the same hand-painted yarns and pattern detailing that to this point have been reserved for adult knitting.

Introduction

THE IDEA of writing this book came to me one dreary, winter afternoon as I was hand painting yarn in my dye studio at Cherry Tree Hill. I recalled my long-ago days of what we called "art" in second grade at Birch Street School, a turn-of-the-century schoolhouse (which has since been torn down) in a small town in rural Maine. Living near the coast, where the gray Maine days were slushy in the early spring and filled with sleet and freezing rain for weeks on end, I spent much time indoors. My favorite part of art, besides the peculiar spearmint smell of the paste we loved to taste, was the big jars of powdered colors the teacher would mix for finger paints. I remember the rainbow spills of bright purple and blue, the prints of small hands and arm rubbings that trailed along the pages of cheap rolled paper, and the spatters of yellow achieved in the end with the flick of a forefinger. Most of all, I recall the look my mother gave me when she saw my face and hair and fingers. People still stare at my fingers.

Messiness aside, I remember the joy of painting without lines or implements and the sheer exhilaration of letting the colors speak for themselves. In this book, I hope to capture that sense of joy and wonder and offer it to you, the hand knitter, in the form of knitted garments created with hand-painted yarns. Watch the colors as they make their own kaleidoscope patterns row by row. Let them stack or shift, form mosaics or not. It's your choice. Choose colors and yarns that suit your personal taste or the taste of the child you knit for. But most of all, let the excitement and creativity of the process transport you.

The projects in this book are grouped into five sections. Each section focuses on a particular fiber and offers a variety of projects. The garments are ordered in complexity from simplest to hardest, but none are rated more difficult than intermediate, and many are at the level of beginner. (Skill levels are based on the Craft Yarn Council guidelines. See page 111.) You will find that most garments are geared toward children in the three- to eight-year-old range. Kids, especially primary-aged children, enjoy the bright rainbow colors offered by painted yarns, so it seemed a natural pairing.

At the beginning of each project, you will find a set of design notes (indicated by a painted sun motif) that grew from questions I asked each designer about their projects. These notes are meant to help knitters understand who the designer is, what yarn and pattern she chose, where her inspiration came from, and why we chose to include the project in this book. It is my hope that these insights help you choose yarn, patterns, and designs for kids outside the scope of this book. We've also included yarn weight icons to help you should you want to substitute yarns. (See page 110 for more information.)

Don't let the ease of these projects put you off. Sweaters don't have to incorporate difficult stitch patterns to be beautiful, nor do they have to adorn the wall to be considered art. These garments are delightful and relaxing to knit and fun for kids to wear. In many cases, the natural fibers, coupled with the brilliant array of colors only painted yarns offer, let the yarn do the work. After all, knitting these projects is just a grown-up version of finger painting.

Knitting with Cottons

COTTON is a breathable alternative to the synthetic yarn found in department stores that too many people often associate with baby wear. It has distinct advantages when knit in children's garments. Cotton is an all-natural fiber that is also easy-care and nonallergenic. Almost every cotton yarn is hand washable and many are machine washable—even yarns painted by hand. Because of its soft hand and durability, cotton is the natural choice for babies—think of the cotton snugglies and receiving blankets that we wrap around newborns. Cotton does not scratch, it provides cool comfort, and unlike other fibers, it can be worn in all seasons. Cotton is an easy choice for beginner knitters because it is a nonslip fiber with a lot of stick on the needle.

There are a few disadvantages to knitting with cotton. Cotton is a heavy fiber, especially when wet, and does not dry as quickly as wool. Cotton tends to stretch, so it is important to use texture, such as garter stitch or slip stitch, when knitting a garment. Or, consider knitting a piece from side to side instead of from the bottom up to prevent the garment from growing. Knitting with preshrunk cotton or mercerized cotton can minimize these problems, and laundering the garments (especially machine drying) helps shrink them back into shape. All in all, the advantages of knitting with and wearing cotton far outweigh the drawbacks.

Very Cherry Vest

By JoAnne Turcotte

This simple project grew from collaboration between JoAnne and me. We wanted a garment that would be easy enough for beginners but still enjoyable for experts—without the look of Knitting 101. JoAnne's self-finishing garter-stitch vest is knit in one piece with no sewing required. Minimal shaping and built-in buttonholes ensure that this vest is simple to knit from start to finish. And using a three-needle bind off at the shoulder seams means that when you're done knitting, you just add buttons and the garment is done! The only stitches needed to complete the entire project are the knit stitch, knit two together, and yarn over.

Wild Cherry is a cheery colorway for this vest. The reds and pinks, with hints of purple, remind us of cherries ready to pick. Small cherry buttons along the front and on the lapels complete the garment. To make this vest a unisex garment, why not try it in the Cabin Fever colorway? The earthy reds and browns, with a hint of charcoal, recall a cozy fireside. Martha's Vineyard is another gender-neutral colorway, with clear blues and greens mixing with the purple of beach plum and sand—an oceanside colorway that neither girls nor boys can resist.

Vital Statistics

Skill Level: Beginner
Children's Sizes: 2 (4, 6, 8, 10, 12)
Finished Chest Measurements: 26 (28½, 30, 32, 34½, 36½)"
Finished Lengths: 13 (14, 15, 15½, 16½, 18)"
Gauge: 16 sts = 4" in garter stitch on US 8 needles

Materials

Yarn is from Cherry Tree Hill.

Yarn: 2 (2, 3, 3, 4, 4) hanks of North Country Cotton (100% cotton; 4 oz/200 yds) in colorway Wild Cherry **3**
Needles: US 8 or size needed to obtain gauge
Notions: 6 buttons (approximately ½" diameter), 3 stitch holders, spare needle

Garter Stitch

Knit all rows.

Vest Instructions

• Loosely CO 106 (116, 122, 130, 140, 148) sts. Work even in garter st for 1", ending with WS row.

• **Next row,** make first buttonhole: K2, K2tog, yo, knit to end of row. Cont making buttonholes every 2 (2, 2½, 2½, 2½, 3)" until there are 4 buttonholes total. AT SAME TIME, cont working in garter st until total length is 6 (7, 8, 8, 9, 10)", ending with WS row.

• **Next row:** K 26 (28, 30, 32, 34, 36). Turn, knit back. Working across this first set of sts only (right front), dec 1 st at armhole edge (end of row) of EOR row 3 (4, 4, 5, 5, 6) times: 23 (24, 26, 27, 29, 30) sts rem.

• Work even until total length is 12 (13, 14, 14½, 15½, 17)", ending with WS row.

• BO 10 (10, 11, 12, 13, 14) sts at beg of next row. Work even for 1". Place rem 13 (14, 15, 15, 16, 16) sts on holder.

• Attach yarn at underarm. BO 3 (4, 4, 4, 4, 4) sts at beg of first row. K 48 (52, 54, 58, 64, 68), counting st already on right needle. Turn, knit back. Working across this second set of sts only (vest back), dec 1 st at each armhole edge (side edge) of EOR row 3 (4, 4, 5, 5, 6) times: 42 (44, 46, 48, 54, 56) sts rem.

• Work even in garter st until total length is same as front: 13 (14, 15, 15½, 16½, 18)". Place sts on holder.

• Attach yarn at underarm. BO 3 (4, 4, 4, 4, 4) sts at beg of first row: 26 (28, 30, 32, 34, 36) sts. Turn, knit back. Working on this last set of sts

Vest shown in Wild Cherry, size 2.

only (left front), dec 1 st at armhole edge EOR 3 (4, 4, 5, 5, 6) times: 23 (24, 26, 27, 29, 30) sts rem.
• Work even until total length is 12 (13, 14, 14½, 15½, 17)", ending with RS row.
• BO 10 (10, 11, 12, 13, 14) sts at beg of next row. Work even for 1". Place rem 13 (14, 15, 15, 16, 16) sts on holder.

Finishing

• Knit shoulder seams tog, using 3-needle BO (see illustrations on page 109). Slide sts from left front shoulder onto left needle. Place sts from back onto right needle. Hold the 2 needles parallel to one another, with right sides of fabric facing. Using third needle, BO same number of sts from both left front and back shoulders simultaneously.
• BO 16 (16, 16, 18, 22, 24) center sts from back needle by themselves for back of neck.
• BO rem sts from right front and back shoulders, using 3-needle BO.
• Fold back lapels. Sew 1 button on each lapel, sewing through both layers to tack lapels in place. Sew rem 4 buttons on left front across from corresponding buttonholes.
• Weave in all ends.

Care

This garment needs only to be blocked very lightly with a steam iron. When soiled, hand or machine wash and either tumble dry or lay flat to dry. The buttons you choose may dictate whether washing needs to be done by hand or not. If you want the convenience of machine washing and drying, be sure to choose washable buttons.

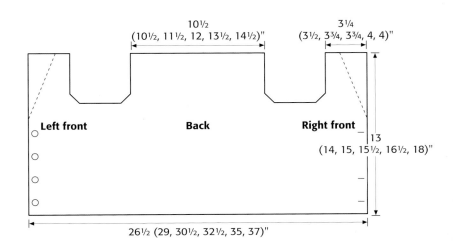

Rainbow Poncho

By JoAnne Turcotte

What child—boy or girl—doesn't love a poncho? This topper is both stylish and quick to knit, and the fringe along the bottom adds a fun finishing touch. The poncho is easy to get on and off and allows full range of movement while providing just enough warmth for that nippy autumn-day romp in the leaves.

In this garment, the stockinette stitch and garter stitch combine to form a pattern called garter-stitch ridge. This simple project requires no shaping; however, you will need to pick up stitches along one edge. Simply pick up one stitch in each stitch along the garter-stitch edge, with no guessing or easing.

Changing color comes into play, as we contrast a hand-dyed solid yarn with a multicolor yarn to achieve a coordinated result. Here, hand-painted Rainbow Cotton provides swirls of subtle color in the recessed areas, while heathery and subtly textured Cotton Bouclé makes the ridges prominent. For this little jeans topper, JoAnne chose neutral shades of the Birches colorway and a heather Loden, so that it could be worn over almost any color.

Vital Statistics

Skill Level: Easy
Children's Sizes: 2–4 (6–8) years
Finished Lengths: 17 (20)"
Gauge: 4 sts = 1" in garter-stitch ridge on US 8 needles

Materials

Yarns are from Cherry Tree Hill.

Yarn:
Color A—2 (3) hanks of Cotton Bouclé (100% cotton; 4 oz/170 yds) in Heather Loden [4]
Color B—1 hank of Rainbow Cotton (99% cotton, 1% nylon binder; 8 oz./400 yds) in colorway Birches [3]
Needles: US 7 and US 8 or size needed to obtain gauge
Notions: Size I crochet hook, tapestry needle

Garter-Stitch Ridge

Row 1 (RS): With color B, knit.
Row 2: Purl.
Row 3: With color A, knit.
Row 4: Knit.
Rep rows 1–4 for patt.

Poncho Instructions

• With color B and larger needles, loosely CO 84 (100) sts.
• Beg with row 1, work in garter-st ridge until total length is 12 (14)", ending with row 4.
• Knit 1 more row with color A. Bind off loosely knitwise with color A.
• Make second piece same as first.

Finishing

• Sew pieces tog as shown in diagram on page 12. After sewing short end of B to BO edge of A, sew remaining short end of A to BO edge of B in same manner.
• With RS facing, using color A and smaller needles, PU 124 (146) sts along lower edge of 1 side of poncho from point at center lower back to point at center front. Knit 4 rows. BO knitwise.
• Rep for other side, PU 3 sts in edging at beg and end of row, plus 124 (146) sts along poncho edge: 130 (152) sts picked up. Knit 4 rows. BO all sts.
• Weave in all ends.
• To make fringe, cut 12" pieces of color A. (You'll need approximately 104 lengths for size 2–4 and 136 lengths for size 6–8.) Holding 2 strands tog, fold fringe pieces in half and pull folded end

Poncho shown is knit in Birches and Heather Loden, size 2–4.

through lower edge of poncho with crochet hook. Pull long ends through loop to secure. Place fringe sections about ¾" apart. Trim fringe so ends are even.

Care

This rugged garment requires very little care. Machine or hand wash and lay flat to dry.

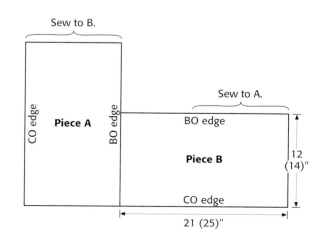

Baby Bouclé Sweater and Hat Set

By JoAnne Turcotte

JoAnne wanted a gender-neutral baby sweater and hat that were easy and quick to knit. She started with the blue and green shades of the Dusk colorway, which work well for both boys and girls. You could achieve a more feminine look by using a colorway rich in pinks and purples, such as Wild Cherry or Winterberry, or a more masculine look with the classic blues and greens of Green Mountain Madness.

This set features garter and stockinette stitches, simple shaping, and shoulders smoothly joined with a three-needle bind off. Add knit 1, purl 1 ribbing, simple sleeves, and a ribbed button band and you have a practical, colorful, and easy-to-knit cardigan. I-cord decorates the top of the hat. The drop-shoulder sleeves are easy to knit and sew in, and combined with wide armhole openings they make for a sweater that is good-looking and easy to put on a baby or young child.

Vital Statistics

Skill Level: Easy
Children's Sizes: 3–6 months (9–12 months, 18 months, 2T, 3T)
Finished Chest Measurements: 20 (22, 24, 26, 28)"
Finished Lengths: 10 (10½, 11½, 12½, 13½)"
Gauge: 16 sts = 4" in stockinette stitch on US 8 needles

Materials

Yarn is from Cherry Tree Hill.

Yarn: 2 (2, 3, 3, 3) hanks of Cotton Bouclé (100% cotton; 4 oz/170 yds) in colorway Dusk (4)
Needles: US 8 or size needed to obtain gauge; US 6, double-pointed; and US 6, 24" circular
Notions: 3 (3, 3, 3, 4) buttons, ⅝" to ¾" diameter; stitch holders; safety pins, tapestry needle

K1, P1 Ribbing

Row 1: P1, *K1, P1; rep from * to end of row.
Row 2: K1, *P1, K1; rep from * to end of row.
Rep rows 1 and 2 for ribbing.

Garter-Stitch Ridge

Row 1 (RS): Knit.
Row 2: Purl.
Row 3: Knit.
Row 4: Knit.

Stockinette Stitch

Knit all RS rows; purl all WS rows.

Sweater Instructions

Back

- With smaller, circular needles, loosely CO 37 (41, 45, 47, 51) sts. Work 1 x 1 ribbing for 6 rows, inc 3 (3, 3, 5, 5) sts evenly across last row: 40 (44, 48, 52, 56) sts.
- Change to larger needles and work rows 1–4 of garter-st ridge 5 times.
- Work in St st until total length measures 10 (10½, 11½, 12½, 13½)", ending with WS row. Place sts on holder.

Right Front

- With smaller, circular needles, loosely CO 19 (21, 23, 23, 25) sts. Work K1, P1 ribbing for 6 rows, inc 1 (1, 1, 3, 3) sts evenly across last row: 20 (22, 24, 26, 28) sts.
- Change to larger needles and work rows 1–4 of garter-st ridge 5 times.
- Work in St st until total length measures 6 (6, 6½, 7, 7½)", ending with WS row.
- Dec 1 st at beg of next row and EOR 5 (6, 7, 8, 9) more times, then at the same edge every following third row 2 times: 12 (13, 14, 15, 16) sts.
- Work even in St st until total length measures same as back, ending with WS row. Place all sts on holder.

Sweater set shown in colorway Dusk, size 3–6 months.

Left Front

• With smaller, circular needles, loosely CO 19 (21, 23, 23, 25) sts. Work K1, P1 ribbing for 6 rows, inc 1 (1, 1, 3, 3) sts evenly across last row: 20 (22, 24, 26, 28) sts.
• Change to larger needles and work rows 1–4 of garter-st ridge 5 times.
• Work in St st until total length measures 6 (6, 6½, 7, 7½)", ending with RS row.
• Dec 1 st at beg of next row and EOR 5 (6, 7, 8, 9) more times, then at the same edge every

following third row 2 times: 12 (13, 14, 15, 16) sts.
• Work even in St st until total length measures same as back, ending with WS row. Place all sts on holder.

Sleeves (Make 2)

• With smaller, circular needles, loosely CO 23 (23, 25, 27, 29) sts. Work K1, P1 ribbing for 6 rows, inc 3 sts evenly across last row: 26 (26, 28, 30, 32) sts.
• Change to larger needles and work rows 1–4 of garter-st ridge 5 times.

• Work in St st, and AT SAME TIME, inc 1 st at each side edge on 3rd row and then on every following 4th row 4 (4, 5, 6, 7) more times: 36 (36, 40, 44, 48) total sts.

• Work even in St st until total length is 6 (6½, 7½, 8½, 9½)", ending with WS row. BO all sts loosely.

Band

• With RS facing, knit shoulder seams tog using 3-needle BO method described on page 109. BO 16 (18, 20, 22, 24) center sts for back neck.

• With smaller, circular needles and RS facing, beg at lower right front edge, PU 27 (27, 30, 32, 35) sts to first neck-shaping dec, PU 19 (22, 24, 27, 29) sts along neck edge to shoulder, PU 16 (18, 20, 22, 24) sts from back neck, PU 19 (22, 24, 27, 29) sts along neck edge to first neck-shaping dec, and PU 26 (26, 29, 31, 34) sts to bottom of sweater: 107 (115, 127, 139, 151) sts.

• Work 1 row of 1 x 1 ribbing, beg with row 2 of rib patt.

• Next row, work buttonholes as follows: Cont in K1, P1 ribbing, working 3 (3, 3, 3, 4) buttonholes (yo, K2tog) evenly spaced along lower left front.

• Work 3 more rows of ribbing. BO in rib patt.

Finishing

• Sew in sleeves.
• Sew side seams and underarm seams.
• Sew buttons to right front band to correspond with buttonholes on left front band.
• Weave in all ends.

Hat Instructions

• With smaller, circular needles, loosely CO 65 (65, 65, 73, 73) sts. Work 1 x 1 ribbing for 6 rows.

• Change to larger needles and work rows 1–4 of garter-st ridge 3 times.

• Work in St st until total length is 5 (5, 5½, 5½, 6)", ending with WS row. Beg dec as follows:

    Row 1: *K6, K2tog; rep across to last st, K1.
    Row 2 and all even-numbered rows: Purl.
    Row 3: *K5, K2tog; rep from * to last st, K1.
    Row 5: *K4, K2tog; rep from * to last st, K1.
    Row 7: *K3, K2tog; rep from * to last st, K1.
    Row 9: *K2, K2tog; rep from * to last st, K1.
    Row 11: *K1, K2tog; rep from * to last st, K1.
    Row 12 (for 3 smaller sizes): P1, *P2tog; rep from * across: 9 sts rem.
    Row 12 (for 2 larger sizes): P3tog, *P2tog; rep from * across: 9 sts rem.

• Divide the 9 sts into 3 groups of 3 sts each. Put 1 group on dpn. Put other 2 groups on safety pins.

• Work 5" of I-Cord on the 3 sts. See "I-Cord" on page 108.

• Secure ends of I-cord by threading yarn through top of hat and tying off end.

• Sew side seam of hat.

• Weave in all ends.

Care

These garments are easy-care cotton. Machine or hand wash and lay flat to dry.

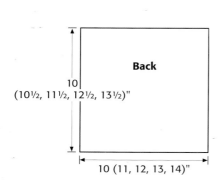

Back
10 (10½, 11½, 12½, 13½)"
10 (11, 12, 13, 14)"

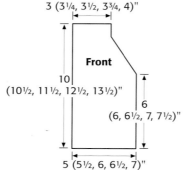

3 (3¼, 3½, 3¾, 4)"
Front
10 (10½, 11½, 12½, 13½)"
6 (6, 6½, 7, 7½)"
5 (5½, 6, 6½, 7)"

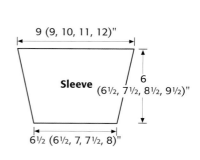

9 (9, 10, 11, 12)"
Sleeve
6 (6½, 7½, 8½, 9½)"
6½ (6½, 7, 7½, 8)"

Cuff-to-Cuff Cardigan

By JoAnne Turcotte

This cardigan is worked in one piece from the left cuff and then across the body, ending at the right cuff. Working side to side is the easiest way to create colorful vertical interest when knitting with hand-painted yarn. There's no noticeable striping or color stacking, and you don't need to switch balls of yarn to get the proper spread of color throughout the garment.

Because this sweater is worked side to side, it requires careful measuring and close adherence to the pattern. You can simplify the job by using safety pins to mark the beginnings and endings of shaped areas and by frequently counting and recording the number of rows. Keeping track of shaping and rows will ensure that the second half of the garment is a mirror image of the first.

The bright and longish repeat of the Peacock colorway works well in a unisex design. The colors have the right energy level for either gender, and the heavy cotton is perfect for spring wear. This garment works just as well in Superwash Merino. For a bolder look, why not try a colorway like Champlain Sunset or Life's a Beach? Both have short, striking repeats.

Vital Statistics

Skill Level: Intermediate
Children's Sizes: 2 (4, 6, 8–10)
Finished Chest Measurements: 24¼ (29, 32, 35¼)"
Finished Lengths: 13 (15, 16, 17)"
Gauge: 16 sts = 4"; 24 rows = 4" in garter-stitch ridge on US 8 needles

Materials

Yarn is from Cherry Tree Hill.

Yarn: 2 (2, 2, 3) hanks of Rainbow Cotton (99% cotton, 1% nylon binder, 8 oz/400 yds) in colorway Peacock (4)
Needles: US 7 and US 8, 24" circular needles, or size needed to obtain gauge
Notions: 5 buttons, ¾" diameter; stitch markers or safety pins, tapestry needle

Garter Stitch

Knit all rows.

Garter-Stitch Ridge

Row 1: Knit.
Row 2: Purl.
Row 3: Knit.
Row 4: Knit.
Rep these 4 rows for patt.

Sweater Instructions

Sweater is knit in one piece from left sleeve to right sleeve.

Left Sleeve

• With smaller needles, CO 32 (32, 36, 36) sts. Work in garter st for 2½ (2½, 3, 3)", ending with WS row.
• Change to larger needles and beg working in garter-st ridge, inc 1 st at each side edge on next and every following 6th row until there are 48 (52, 56, 60) sts. Cont even in patt until piece measures 12 (13½, 15, 16½)", ending with WS row. Make note of number of rows worked even to achieve this length. Cut yarn.

Cardigan shown in colorway Peacock, size 10.

Left Side

• Leaving sleeve sts on left needle, CO 28 (34, 36, 38) sts on right needle for back. Join to sts already on needle as follows: Work 24 (26, 28, 30) sts of sleeve, PM to designate shoulder, work remaining 24 (26, 28, 30) sleeve sts, CO 28 (34, 36, 38) sts for front: 104 (120, 128, 136) sts.

• Work even for 3¾ (4¼, 5, 5½)", ending with WS row.

• **Front neck shaping:** On next row, work to marker. Remove marker. Attach second ball of yarn and BO 2 (1, 1, 1) sts, work rest of row. Work both front and back at same time, using separate balls of yarn.

• **Next row and all WS rows of neck shaping:** Work to 2 sts before front neck edge, work 2 sts tog. Shape as foll for size you're making:

  Size 2: BO 2 sts on next 3 RS rows. End with WS row for total of 6 rows worked and 10 sts dec: 42 sts rem for front.

  Size 4: BO 1 st at neck edge of next 4 RS rows. End with WS row for total of 10 rows worked and 10 sts dec: 50 sts rem for front.

  Sizes 6 and 8–10: BO 1 st at neck edge of next 2 RS rows, then BO 2 sts at beg of foll 2 RS rows. End with WS row for total of 10 rows worked and 12 sts dec: 52 (56) sts rem for front.

  All sizes: Work 8 (8, 8, 10) rows even. On next row, BO all front sts. Cut yarn.

Right Side

- With back sts on right needle and second ball of yarn, CO 42 (50, 52, 56) sts. Then, working WS row, work across these CO sts. Cont, working 7 (9, 9, 11) more rows on both right front and back with separate balls of yarn, ending on RS.
- Over next 6 (10, 10, 10) rows, reverse left front neck shaping: CO sts on RS rows and inc 1 st on each WS row.
- Work across all 104 (120, 128, 136) sts, rejoining front to back at neck edge. Cut off extra ball of yarn. Work even for 3¾ (4¼, 5, 5½)", ending with WS row.

Right Sleeve

- On next row, BO 28 (34, 36, 38) sts, work to end of row. Turn and BO 28 (34, 36, 38) sts: 48 (52, 56, 60) sts rem for sleeve.
- Work right sleeve even for same number of rows as were worked even at top of left sleeve. (This is number of rows you were instructed to note.)
- Dec 1 st on each edge every 6th row until 32 (32, 36, 36) sts rem. Work 5 rows even.
- Change to smaller needles, work in garter st for 2½ (2½, 3, 3)", ending with WS row. BO all sts.

Finishing

- Sew side seams and underarm sleeve seams, reversing seams at cuffs since they will be turned up.
- **Neck edge:** With smaller needles and RS facing, PU 56 (59, 63, 65) sts around neck edge. Work 3 rows in garter st. BO all sts.
- **Bottom edge:** With larger needles and RS facing, PU 88 (100, 112, 126) sts around bottom edge. Work 7 rows in garter st. BO all sts.
- **Button band** (left for girls, right for boys): With smaller needles and RS facing, PU 46 (52, 54, 56) sts along front edge. Work 7 rows in garter st. BO all sts.
- **Buttonhole band** (right for girls, left for boys): With smaller needles and RS facing, PU 46 (52, 54, 56) sts along front edge. Work 3 rows in garter st. **Next row:** Work 5 buttonholes (yo, K2tog) evenly spaced along row. Top buttonhole should be ½" from top of sweater. Work 3 more rows in garter st. BO all sts.
- Weave in all ends.
- Sew buttons to band to correspond with buttonholes.
- Fold up sleeve cuffs.

Care

Machine wash, lay flat to dry.

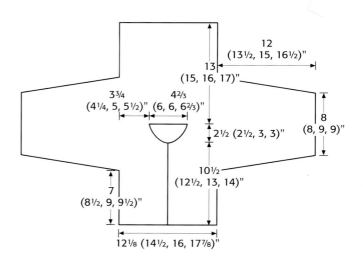

Sweetheart Sweater Set

By JoAnne Turcotte

The Baby Bouclé set on page 13 is simple, elegant, and fast to work up. Wanting those same characteristics in a little girl's outfit, JoAnne came up with the Sweetheart Sweater Set. A ruffled edge on the sweater and hat and simple lacework hearts on the sweater fronts add a frilliness that any little girl will love. This little lady's sweetheart sweater called for a pastel colorway. We chose Country Garden, because it reminded us of spring flowers.

Working the heart lace motif requires reading a simple chart. To make following the lace chart trouble-free, place stitch markers on both sides of the stitch area where the lace will be worked before working the first charted row. Be sure to count the stitches so that they correspond to the stitches on the chart. Each row ends with the same number of stitches it started with. Yarn overs, which are used in many of our garments to create buttonholes, are used here to create the easy openwork pattern. The ruffle is easier than it looks as well—just cast on twice the number of stitches required for the sweater body, then decrease them away a few rows later.

Vital Statistics

Skill Level: Intermediate
Children's Sizes: 3–6 months (9–12 months, 18 months, 2T, 3T)
Finished Chest Measurements: 20 (22, 24, 26, 28)"
Gauge: 16 sts = 4" in stockinette stitch on US 8 needles

Materials

Yarn is by Cherry Tree Hill.

Yarns: 2 (2, 3, 3, 3) hanks of Cotton Bouclé (100% cotton; 4 oz/170 yds) in colorway Country Garden 🄴
Needles: US 6 and US 8 or size needed to obtain gauge
Notions: 4 (4, 5, 5, 5) buttons, ½" diameter; stitch markers or safety pins; elastic thread (optional); tapestry needle

Stockinette Stitch

Knit all RS rows; purl all WS rows.

Garter Stitch

Knit all rows.

Sweater Instructions

The sweater sections are worked separately and then sewn together.

Back

• With larger needles, loosely CO 80 (88, 96, 104, 112) sts. Purl 2 rows.
• **Next row (RS):** Beg with knit row, work 4 rows of St st.
• **Next row (RS):** Change to smaller needles and K2tog across: 40 (44, 48, 52, 56) sts. Knit 3 rows.
• Change to larger needles and work in St st until total length measures 10 (10½, 11½, 12½, 13½)", ending with WS row. BO all sts.

Right Front

• With larger needles, loosely CO 40 (44, 48, 52, 56) sts. Purl 2 rows.
• **Next row (RS):** Beg with knit row, work 4 rows of St st.
• **Next row (RS):** Change to smaller needles and K2tog across: 20 (22, 24, 26, 28) sts. Knit 3 rows.
• Change to larger needles and work in St st for 4 (6, 6, 8, 8) rows, ending with WS row.
• **Set up chart:** Work 2 (3, 4, 4, 4) sts in St st, PM, work chart across next 15 sts, PM, work in St st to end of row. Work rest of chart as established.
• Once chart is complete, cont in St st until piece measures 7½ (7½, 8½, 9½, 10½)" or is 12 (14,

Sweater set shown in colorway Country Garden, size 9–12 months.

14, 14, 14) rows shorter than back, ending with WS row.

Sweetheart Sweater Lace Chart

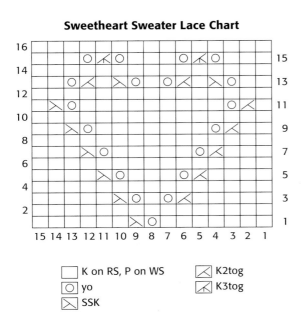

Legend:
- ☐ K on RS, P on WS
- ○ yo
- ⧄ SSK
- ⧅ K2tog
- ⧆ K3tog

• BO 4 (4, 5, 5, 5) sts at beg of next row. Work 1 row even. Dec 1 st at beg of next row and every foll RS row 4 (5, 5, 5, 5) times total: 12 (13, 14, 16, 18) sts rem.

• Work even in St st until total length measures same as back, ending with WS row. BO all sts.

Left Front

• With larger needles, loosely CO 40 (44, 48, 52, 56) sts. Purl 2 rows.

• **Next row (RS):** Beg with knit row, work 4 rows of St st.

• **Next row (RS):** Change to smaller needles and K2tog across: 20 (22, 24, 26, 28) sts. Knit 3 rows.

• Change to larger needles and work in St st for 4 (6, 6, 8, 8) rows, ending with WS row.

• **Set up chart:** Work 3 (4, 5, 7, 9) sts in St st, PM, work chart across next 15 sts, PM, work in St st to end of row. Work rest of chart.

• Cont in St st until piece measures 7½ (7½, 8½, 9½, 10½)" or is 11 (13, 13, 13, 13) rows shorter than back, ending with RS row.

• BO 4 (4, 5, 5, 5) sts at beg of next row. Work 1 row even. Dec 1 st at beg of next row and every foll WS row 4 (5, 5, 5, 5) times total: 12 (13, 14, 16, 18) sts rem.

• Work even in St st until total length measures same as back, ending with WS row. BO all sts.

Sleeves (Make 2)

• With larger needles, loosely CO 46 (46, 50, 54, 58) sts. Purl 2 rows.

• **Next row (RS):** Beg with knit row, work 4 rows of St st.

• **Next row (RS):** Change to smaller needles and K2tog across: 23 (23, 25, 27, 29) sts. Knit 3 rows.

• Change to larger needles and work in St st, AT SAME TIME inc 1 st at each edge on 5th and every foll 4th row 6 (7, 8, 9, 9) times total: 35 (37, 41, 45, 47) sts.

• Cont to work even in St st until total length is 6½ (7, 7½, 8½, 9)", ending with WS row. BO all sts.

Finishing

• Sew shoulder seams together.

• Sew in sleeves. Sew side seams and sleeve seams.

• **Neckband:** With smaller needles and RS facing, PU 16 (18, 20, 21, 21) sts along right neck edge, PU 16 (18, 20, 20, 20) sts across back neck, PU 16 (18, 20, 21, 21) sts along left neck edge: 48 (54, 60, 62, 62) sts. Work in garter st for 4 rows. BO all sts.

• **Buttonhole band:** With smaller needles and RS facing, PU 37 (41, 45, 49, 53) sts along right front edge. Knit 1 row. Next row: Knit, working 4 (4, 5, 5, 5) buttonholes (yo, K2tog) evenly spaced from ½" below neck edge to top of ruffle. Work 2 more rows in garter st. BO all sts.

• **Button band:** With smaller needles and RS facing, PU 37 (41, 45, 49, 53) sts along left front edge. Work 4 rows garter st. BO all sts.

• Weave in all ends.

• Sew buttons on left button band to correspond with buttonholes on right band.

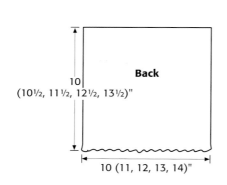

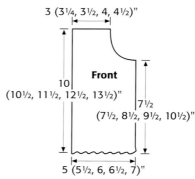

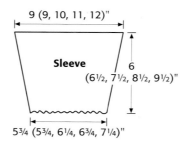

Hat Instructions

• With larger needles, loosely CO 114 (130, 130, 146, 146) sts. Purl 2 rows.

• **Next row (RS):** Beg with knit row, work 4 rows of St st.

• **Next row (RS):** Change to smaller needles and K2tog across: 57 (65, 65, 73, 73) sts. Knit 3 rows.

• Change to larger needles and work in St st until total length is 5 (5, 5½, 5½, 6)", ending with WS row. Begin dec:

    Row 1: *K6, K2tog, rep from * to last st, K1.

    Row 2 and even-numbered rows: Purl.

    Row 3: *K5, K2tog, rep from * to last st, K1.

    Row 5: *K4, K2tog, rep from * to last st, K1.

    Row 7: *K3, K2tog, rep from * to last st, K1.

    Row 9: *K2, K2tog, rep from * to last st, K1.

    Row 11: *K1, K2tog, rep from * to last st, K1.

    Row 12: P1, *P2tog, rep from * across.

• Cut yarn, leaving 18" tail. Thread yarn through rem sts, draw up tightly, and anchor yarn on inside of hat.

• Sew side seam of hat and weave in all ends.

• *Optional:* If hat is too loose on head, use darning needle to weave strand of elastic thread through sts along garter ridge at top of ruffle. Adjust to fit.

Care

Machine wash, lay flat to dry.

The same sweater and cap knit in colorway African Grey looks more grown-up and is lovely paired with a lavender turtleneck.

Knitting with Washable Wools

WOOL remains the natural fiber choice for many knitters, but it is not always the first choice for children's wear. Although it is a breathable fiber that provides lightweight warmth, many knitters avoid wool and other animal fibers for children because they have a tendency to scratch and are not machine washable. Enter the new generation of washable wools called Superwash. These sturdy yarns are machine washable and can even go into the dryer with minimal shrinkage. Better yet, most of them are spun from merino or other soft wools that provide the breathable warmth of wool without the scratchiness. Even many children who are plagued by wool allergies have no adverse reaction to Superwash wools.

Like most animal-fiber yarns, washable wool is durable and resilient. Even when stretched out of shape, it has memory and will bounce back to its original dimensions after washing. Wool is an easy choice for beginner knitters because it is not too slippery on the needles.

It's hard to think of any disadvantages to knitting garments for children from washable wool. However, by its very nature, wool tends to be warmer than cotton and is not an all-season fiber.

Little Leggings and Watch Cap

By Judy Sumner

Supersock Merino is a popular, fingering-weight, luxury sock yarn. Its softness and elasticity, combined with rugged wash-and-wear durability, make it perfect for leggings that need to stretch and bend with a toddler. We wanted a roomy, unisex garment with matching hat that would be easy and fun to knit. These quick-knit garments are designed with enough ease to grow with the child. Both pieces are knit in the round on circular and double-pointed needles, with no seams other than the crotch, which is grafted together.

These lightweight, cozy garments are perfect for small heads and chubby legs. Toddlers will have no problem pulling up the elastic-waist leggings and popping the hat on or off their heads. There's even plenty of diaper room built in!

Green Mountain Madness is a classic colorway of bright blues and greens, adding playfulness without being gender-specific. The colorway has universal appeal and would look great on any child. For different looks, try the Champlain Sunset or Peacock colorways.

Vital Statistics

Skill Level: Intermediate
Children's Sizes: 2T (3T, 4T)
Finished Waist Measurements: 22 (23, 23¾)"
Finished Leg Length (from crotch): 14½ (14½, 15)"
Finished Cap Circumference: 18 (18½, 19)"
Gauge: 28 sts = 4"; 8 rounds = 1" in stockinette stitch on US 3 needles

Materials

Yarn is by Cherry Tree Hill.

Yarn: 2 hanks of Supersock Merino (100% wool; 4 oz/370 yards) in colorway Green Mountain Madness **[1]**
Needles: US 3 double-pointed and 16" and 24" circular needles or size needed to obtain gauge
Notions: Stitch markers, stitch holders, safety pin, ¾ yard of ¾"-wide elastic for waist of leggings, decorative button for cap (optional), tapestry needle

Stockinette Stitch

Knit all RS rows; purl all WS rows.

K2, P2 Ribbing

Multiple of 4

All rows: *K2, P2, rep from * to end.

Leggings Instructions

Abbreviations: SSK (modified) Place needle in front of first st and in back of next st, and work 2 sts tog, dec 1 st.
• With 24" circular needles, CO 154 (160, 166) sts. Join, being careful not to twist sts; PM. Work ¾" of K1, P1 ribbing for casing. Purl 1 rnd (for turn or fold-over row of waistband) and then work another ¾" of K1, P1 ribbing.
• Change to St st and work for 2 (2½, 3)".
• **Inc rnds:** K 75 (78, 81), inc in next st (knit in front and back of stitch), PM, K2, PM, inc 1 in next st; knit rem sts in rnd.
• Knit 3 rnds.
• Cont to inc every 4th rnd (before first marker and after second marker) until total of 10 inc rnds have been worked: 20 inc sts—174 (180, 186) sts.
• Cont in St st until piece measures approximately 7 (7½, 8)" from turn row on casing; place last 5 sts of rnd on stitch holder.

Leggings shown in
Green Mountain
Madness, size 2T.

Separate for Legs

When there are too few sts for circular needle,
change to dpn.

• K6 and place these sts on same holder as 5 sts
from previous rnd. These are crotch sts.

• Change to 16" circular needles and K 77
(80, 83).

• Place next 10 sts on another holder for crotch
stitches.

• Transfer sts still on 24" needles to a piece of
yarn for right leg and secure ends, or leave them
on spare needle.

• **Left leg:** Join sts on 16" needle (at crotch) to

form rnd, PM, and work around 77 (80, 83) sts
for leg.

• **Next rnd:** K 2 (0, 2) tog and complete rnd: 76
(80, 82) sts. Knit 3 more rnds.

• **Dec rnd:** K2tog, knit to last 3 sts before marker,
SSK, K1 (2 sts dec on rnd). Knit next 5 rnds. Rep
until 6 (6, 8) dec rnds have been completed and
then dec every 4th rnd until 48 sts rem. Work
even in St st until legs measure 9½ (10¾, 11¼)"
or desired length from crotch.

• Change to K2, P2 ribbing for 4". BO in ribbing.

• **Right leg:** Rep as for left leg, reversing shaping:
With back of leggings facing you, K1, K2tog, knit
to last 2 sts of rnd, SSK.

Finishing

• Graft crotch stitches using the kitchener stitch (see page 108).
• Measure child's waist and cut elastic 1" longer than waist measurement. Fold casing along row of purl sts and sew edge in place by hand, leaving last 2" open. Put safety pin on one end of elastic and feed through casing. Lap ends of elastic by ½" and sew securely. Complete sewing on casing.

Care

This garment needs to be blocked only very lightly with a steam iron. When soiled, hand or machine wash and tumble dry or lay flat to dry.

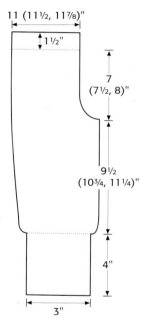

Shown in colorway Green Mountain Madness, size 2T. Cap has a lot of stretch, so size is approximate.

Cap Instructions

• With 16" circular needles, CO 132 (140, 152) sts. Join, being careful not to twist sts.
• Work K2, P2 ribbing until work measures 6¼ (6¾, 7½)" from beg.
• **Next rnd:** Change to St st and dec 2 (0, 2) sts.
• Knit 1 rnd.
• Shape top of cap, changing to dpn when too few sts remain for circular needle:

    K8, K2tog around. Knit 1 rnd even.
    K7, K2tog around. Knit 1 rnd even.
    K6, K2tog around. Knit 1 rnd even.
    K5, K2tog around. Knit 1 rnd even.
    K4, K2tog around. Knit 1 rnd even.
    K3, K2tog around. Knit 1 rnd even.
    K2, K2tog around. Knit 1 rnd even.
    K1, K2tog around. Knit 1 rnd even.
    K2tog around.

• Weave tail through rem sts and pull tightly. If you are using a decorative button, sew it on with yarn tail and then fasten off. If you are not using a button, pull tail to inside top of cap and anchor.

Socks—His, Hers, and Ours

By JoAnne Turcotte

Every child deserves several pairs of simply and lovingly knit socks. Easy to put on and fun to wear, these kid-happy socks knit quickly from soft, washable wool that keeps toes toasty. Color can lend a masculine tilt (His) or a feminine flair (Hers). Still other colors in the hand-paint collection blend so well that they are right for either sex (Ours), resulting in socks that can be handed down from brother to sister or vice versa.

Knitting socks requires the use of double-pointed needles so that you can knit in the round without seams. These needles also produce the shaping of heels and toes. Simple short-row shaping is also used to form the heel. The good news is these short rows are far easier to accomplish than you might think!

Since knitting the same sock style repeatedly can be less than exciting, we offer you five different sock tops to beat the boredom. Here's another tip to make knitting two of the same item go quickly: Before starting, divide the yarn in half and, using two sets of double-pointed needles, begin both socks at the same time. Knit one cuff, then the other. Knit one heel, then the other, and so on. Before you know it, both socks will be finished!

Vital Statistics

Skill Level: Intermediate
Children's Sizes: 6–12 months (12–24 months, 2T–4T)
Gauge: 24 sts = 4" in stockinette stitch on US 5 needles

Materials

Yarn is by Cherry Tree Hill.

Yarn: 1 hank of Supersport sock yarn (100% washable wool; 4 oz/250 yds) in color of choice (2)
Needles: 1 set of US 5 double-pointed needles or size needed to obtain gauge
Notions: Split-ring markers, tapestry needle

Sock Instructions

Note: When slipping stitches, always slip as if to purl, except for the SKP.
SKP: Sl 1 st as if to knit, sl next st as if to purl, insert left needle into sts from left to right and knit the 2 sts tog.

Cuff

Except for Ruffled Sock, CO 24 (32, 40) sts. Divide sts onto 3 needles. Being careful not to twist sts, join and mark beg of rnd.

Basic Ribbed Cuff (His)
Shown in Fall Foliage

• **Rnd 1:** *K2, P2, rep from * around.
• Rep rnd 1, working in K2, P2 ribbing until total length is 3½ (4½, 5)", ending at beg of rnd.
• Finish, using basic heel and foot instructions on page 34.

Tracks Pattern (His)
Shown in Life's a Beach

• Work K1, P1 ribbing for 5 rnds.
• Tracks patt:
  Rnds 1 and 2: Knit.
  Rnds 3 and 4: *K2, P2; rep from * around.
• Work in tracks patt until total length is 3½ (4½, 5)", ending with rnd 4.
• Finish, using basic heel and foot instructions on page 34.

Lace Pattern (Hers)
Shown in Winterberry

• Lace patt:
  Rnd 1: P1, *(K2, P2); rep from * to last 3 sts, K2, P1.
  Rnd 2: *P1, yo, SSK, P1; rep from * to end of rnd.
  Rnd 3: Rep rnd 1.
  Rnd 4: *P1, K2tog, yo, P1; rep from * to end of rnd.

These socks provide you with enough options to clothe youngsters in socks for their entire childhood. From left, the socks are **Cable Twist** (in colorway Quarry Hill), **Ruffled** (in colorway Country Garden), **Tracks** (in colorway Life's a Beach), **Basic Ribbed Cuff** (in colorway Fall Foliage), and **Lace** (in colorway Winterberry).

• Work in lace patt until total length is 3½ (4½, 5)", ending with rnd 1 or 3.

• Finish, using basic heel and foot instructions on page 34.

Ruffled Sock (Hers)

Shown in Country Garden

• Cast on 96 (128, 160) sts. Divide sts onto 3 needles. Being careful not to twist sts, join and work in the round as foll:
   • **Rnd 1:** Knit.
   • **Rnd 2:** P2tog around: 48 (64, 80) sts.
   • **Rnd 3:** Purl.
   • **Rnd 4:** *P2tog, P2tog tbl; rep from * to end of rnd: 24 (32, 40) sts.
   • **Rnd 5:** Knit.
• **Next rnd:** Work in *K2, P2; rep from * around. Cont to work in K2, P2 ribbing for 3 (3½, 4)", ending at beg of rnd.

• Finish, using basic heel and foot instructions on page 34.

Cable Twist Pattern (Ours)

Shown in Quarry Hill

• Cable twist right patt:
   Rnd 1: *K2, P2; rep from * around.
   Rnd 2: *Twist 2R (knit next 2 sts tog but do not slip sts from needle, then knit first st again, taking both sts off needle at once), P2; rep from * around.
   Rnd 3: *K2, P2; rep from * around.
• Rep rnds 1–3 for cable twist pattern. Work in patt until total length is 3½ (4½, 5)", ending with rnd 1.
• Finish, using basic heel and foot instructions on page 34.

Heel Flap (All Socks)

• Work 3 rnds in St st (knit every rnd).
• **Next rnd, divide sts for heel:** Transfer sts around so there are 12 (16, 20) sts on first needle and 6 (8, 10) sts on each of other 2 needles. Work back and forth across FIRST NEEDLE ONLY as follows:

> **Row 1:** Sl 1, knit across.
> **Row 2:** Sl 1, purl across.
> Rep these 2 rows for 12 (16, 20) rows total, then work row 1 once more. The heel will be 13 (17, 21) rows long.

Heel Turn (All Socks)

• **Row 1:** Sl 1, P 6 (8, 10), P2tog, P1, turn.
• **Row 2:** Sl 1, K3, K2tog, K1, turn.
• **Row 3:** Sl 1, purl to 1 st before last turn (you'll see a small gap where last turn was), P2tog, P1, turn.
• **Row 4:** Sl 1, knit to 1 st before last turn (look for gap), K2tog, K1, turn.
• Rep rows 3 and 4 until all sts at ends are used up, ending with RS row: 8 (10, 12) sts rem.

Gusset (All Socks)

• Working with same needle, PU 7 (9, 11) sts along side of heel (sts on needle 1). Use another needle to knit across all sts from next 2 needles (sts are now on needle 2).

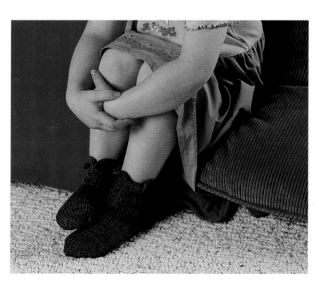

• Using a spare needle, PU 7 (9, 11) sts along other side of heel and cont knitting to center of heel sts: 4 (5, 6) sts (sts now on needle 3). There should now be 11 (14, 17) sts on needles 1 and 3, and 12 (16, 20) sts on needle 2. Center of heel is beg of rnd; needle 2 contains instep sts. Beg dec as foll:

> **Rnd 1:** Knit.
> **Rnd 2:** Knit to within 3 sts of end of first needle, K2tog, K1. Knit across second needle. On third needle, K1, SKP, knit to end.
> Rep rnds 1 and 2 until there are 6 (8, 10) sts left on both needles 1 and 3. Needle 2 will remain at 12 (16, 20) sts since no dec takes place there. You will now be back to original number of sts: 24 (32, 40) sts.

• Knit all rnds in St st until total length from back of heel is 1 (1½, 1½)" shorter than desired length of finished sock or about 3 (3½, 4½)".

Toe Shaping (All Socks)

• Rearrange sts on needles, if necessary, so there are now 6 (8, 10) sts on each of needles 1 and 3, and 12 (16, 20) sts on needle 2. Beg of rnd is still at center back of heel. Beg dec as foll:

> **Rnd 1:** On needle 1, knit to last 3 sts, K2tog, K1. On needle 2, K1, SKP, knit to last 3 sts, K2tog, K1. On needle 3, K1, SKP, knit to end (center of heel).
> **Rnd 2:** Knit.
> Rep rnds 1 and 2 until there are 12 sts left: 3 sts on needles 1 and 3; 6 sts on needle 2.

Finishing

• Use kitchener stitch (see page 108) to weave toe. Anchor yarn end on inside and weave in ends.
• Make a second sock, counting rows to make sure it is same length as first one.

Care

Machine wash and tumble dry. Washable wool produces socks that wear well and hold their shape.

Take It from the Top Poncho

By Donna Druchunas

Talk about a blast from the past! The last poncho that designer Donna Druchunas wore was one her grandmother knit for her in 1969. But ponchos are back in fashion, and this updated version is shown in bold stripes. The trick with stripes is to choose colorways that contrast rather than match, since like colors tend to blur the design lines. Here, Silver Streak, a simple black-and-white colorway, contrasts sharply with the saturated shades of Tropical Storm to define the stripes. And the colors are suitable for both boys and girls.

This poncho is as kid-friendly as they come. The one-size pattern can be knit to any length, and it can even be lengthened at any time to grow with the child. The drawstring, trimmed with pompoms, lets you adjust it to fit a child of any size.

The trickiest part of this project is getting started. After knitting a strip for one side of the first round, you'll need to pick up stitches along one short end of the strip and then cast on more stitches to work the next part of the round. Once you've got that mastered, the rest is easy.

Vital Statistics

Skill Level: Easy
Size: One size fits all. Work to desired length.
Gauge: 4 sts = 1" in garter stitch on US 9 needles

Materials

Yarns are by Cherry Tree Hill.

Yarn:
MC—3 hanks of Super Worsted Merino (100% washable wool; 4 oz/188 yds) in Tropical Storm (4)
CC—3 hanks of Super Worsted Merino in Silver Streak (4)
Needles: US 9, 29" circular needles, or size needed to obtain gauge and US 7, 16" circular needles
Notions: 1½" plastic pom-pom maker or cardboard, tapestry needle

Garter Stitch (MC)

Knit all rows.

Garter Slip Stitch (CC)

Rows 1 and 2: Knit.
Row 3 (RS): *K1, wyib sl 1 pw; rep from * to last 2 sts, K2.
Row 4 (WS): K2, *wyif sl 1 pw, K1; rep from * to end of row.
Rep rows 1–4 for pattern.

Poncho Instructions

The poncho is worked in striped rounds by knitting strips and then picking up stitches on the end of the strip until four strips are joined to form a square.

Stripe 1

• With MC and larger needles, CO 20 sts. Work 20 rows in garter st (10 ridges).
• BO 19 sts: 1 st rem. Side 1 is complete.
• PU 9 sts along short end of work adjacent to st still on needle. When you reach end of row, CO 20 sts: 30 sts total.
• Work 20 rows in garter st (10 ridges).
• BO 29 sts: 1 st rem. Side 2 is complete.
• PU 9 sts along short end of work adjacent to st still on needle. When you reach end of row, CO 20 sts: 30 sts total.
• Work 20 rows in garter st (10 ridges).
• BO 29 sts: 1 st rem. Side 3 is complete.

The color scheme in this poncho is an example of coordinating two different multicolor yarns. Note that Tropical Storm and Silver Streak contrast with each other enough to make the stripes stand out, but not to the point of distraction.

• PU 9 sts along short end of work adjacent to st still on needle. When you reach end of row, CO 20 sts and then PU 10 sts from short end of side 1 to form a square: 40 sts total. Take care not to twist the strips as you join them.
• Work 20 rows in garter st (10 ridges).
• BO 39 sts.

Stripe 2

Change to CC and work in garter slip stitch.
• Pick up 39 sts along side 1 of rnd 1: 40 sts total.
• Work 20 rows in patt (5-patt rep).
• BO 39 sts: 1 st rem. Side 1 is complete.
• PU 49 sts along side 2 of stripe 1: 50 sts total.
• Work 20 rows in patt (5-patt rep).
• BO 49 sts: 1 st rem. Side 2 is complete.

• PU 49 sts along side 3 of stripe 1: 50 sts total.
• Work 20 rows in patt (5-patt rep).
• BO 49 sts: 1 st rem. Side 3 is complete.
• PU 59 sts along side 4 of strip 1: 60 sts total.
• Work 20 rows in patt (5-patt rep).
• BO 59 sts.

Stripe 3

Change to MC and work in garter st.
• PU 59 sts along side 1 of stripe 2: 60 sts total.
• Work 20 rows (10 ridges).
• BO 59 sts: 1 st rem. Side 1 is complete.
• PU 69 sts along side 2 of stripe 2: 70 sts total.
• Work 20 rows (10 ridges).
• BO 69 sts: 1 st rem. Side 2 is complete.
• PU 69 sts along side 3 of stripe 2: 70 sts total.

- Work 20 rows (10 ridges).
- BO 69 sts: 1 st rem. Side 3 is complete.
- PU 79 sts along side 4 of stripe 2: 80 sts total.
- Work 20 rows (10 ridges).
- BO 79 sts.

Additional Stripes

- Rep stripes 2 and 3, picking up 20 more sts on each side than for stripe before, until poncho is desired length (see illustration below right for stitch count).
- BO all rem sts.

Collar

Adding the collar changes the top edge from a square into a rounded neckline.
- Choose a corner for the center front. Beg here with RS facing, using MC and smaller needles to PU 80 sts evenly spaced around neck opening. Do not join.
- Working back and forth to leave opening in collar, knit 3 rows.
- **Next row (RS):** Work eyelet row as foll: K4, *K4, yo, K2tog, K3; rep from * to last 4 sts, K4.
- **Next row (WS):** Knit.
- Work in ribbing until collar measures 3" or desired length as foll:

    RS rows: K1, *K2, P2; rep from * to last 3 sts, K3.

    WS rows: K1, *P2, K2; rep from * to last 3 sts, P2, K1.

- BO loosely in rib patt.

Finishing

- Weave in ends.

Pom-pom (Make 2)

Use a 1½" plastic pom-pom maker or make your own by cutting out 2 doughnut-shaped pieces of cardboard 1½" in diameter. Then cut out a ½"-diameter circle from the center of each cardboard circle.
- Use several strands of CC to make pom-poms, referring to page 109.

Drawstring

- Cut 3 strands of CC approximately 90" long. Knot strands tog at both ends.
- Attach 1 end of strands to hook or doorknob, or ask someone to hold onto end for you. Twist other end in clockwise direction until it's tightly twisted and begins to kink.
- Grasp center of cord and fold it in half so knotted ends are even. Let go of center and allow cord to twist back on itself.
- Smooth out cord. Tie new knot at each end of cord, then cut off smaller knots on one end and cut open other folded end.
- Weave drawstring through eyelets in collar and sew pom-pom onto each end.

Care

Wash poncho before wearing. This will relax the garment and make the poncho softer and more comfortable. Machine wash on a gentle cycle in cold water and dry in low-temperature dryer.

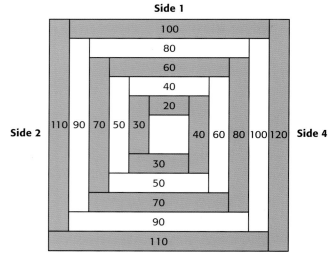

Take It from the Top Pullovers

By Donna Druchunas

This duo of top-down pullovers is designed to be easy to adapt for boys or girls and to work well as a hand-me-down long into the future. We chose colorways that could be considered unisex and then added a twist, literally, to one of the sweaters. The girl's version is knit in a more complex colorway, and to prevent the stitch pattern from overpowering the colors the pattern was kept simple. Conversely, we knit the boy's version in subtler, monochromatic browns so that the more complex cable stitch would be the star.

There's no need to fret about dirt from the playground or lunchroom with these kid-proof sweaters knit from wash-and-wear merino. Just toss the sweaters in the washer and dryer and they come out like new. The hand-painted colorways help hide any stains, too! However, make sure to wash your swatch before starting the sweater. Superwash wool opens up quite a bit when washed. If an exact fit is needed, don't trust the gauge of an unwashed swatch. On the other hand, it shouldn't be a problem if a kid's sweater comes out a little too big. It will just fit better next year.

Vital Statistics

Skill Level: Intermediate
Children's Sizes: 4 (6, 8, 10)
Finished Chest Measurements: 26 (28, 30½, 32½)"
Gauge: 5.25 sts and 8 rows = 1" in garter-check rib or garter-check cable on US 7 needles

Materials

Yarn is by Cherry Tree Hill.

Yarn: 2 (3, 3, 4) hanks of Superwash Merino DK (100% merino wool; 4 oz/280 yds), in colorway Blueberry Hill (Girl's) or Java (Boy's) **3**
Needles: US 7 or size needed to obtain gauge and US 5, 20" circular
Notions: Stitch markers, cable needle (boy's version only), stitch holders, tapestry needle

Garter-Check Rib (shown on girl's version)

Multiple of 12 + 4 sts

Rows 1, 3, 5, and 7 (RS): Knit.
Rows 2, 4, and 6 (WS): P4, *K8, P4; rep from * to end.
Row 8: Purl.
Rep rows 1–8 for patt.

Garter-Check Cable (shown on boy's version)

Multiple of 12 + 4 sts

Rows 1, 3, and 5 (RS): Knit.
Rows 2, 4, and 6 (WS): *P4, K8. Rep from * to last 4 sts, P4.
Row 7: *4-st right cable (slip 2 sts to cable needle and hold in back, K2, K2 from cable needle), K8; rep from * to last 4 sts, 4-st right cable.
Row 8: Purl.
Rep rows 1–8 for patt.

Edge Pattern Stitch

Rows 1–7: Knit.
Row 8 (WS): Purl.
Rep rows 1–8 for patt.

Sweater Instructions

Note: These two sweaters are almost identical. At several points in your knitting, you will need to make choices about the design. The project directions give instructions for all options.

1. Before you start, choose a pattern stitch (see pattern stitch directions above).
2. Determine which type of bottom edge to use. The girl's version has a tunic edge, with front and back being worked the same. The boy's

Boy's version is shown in colorway Java, size 4, and girl's sweater above is shown in colorway Blueberry Hill, size 6.

version has a shirttail edge, where the back is approximately 2" longer than the front.

3. Choose a collar. The girl's version features a rolled neck, while the boy's version has a hemmed crew neck.

Back

• With larger needles, CO 68 (74, 80, 86) sts. This is the shoulder edge, not the bottom!
• **Set-up row:** K2 (5, 8, 11), PM, work in patt st of choice for 64 sts, PM, K2 (5, 8, 11).
• Work even in patt, working sts outside of markers in edge patt st. Slip markers whenever you come to them.
• When piece measures 6 (7, 7, 7½)", PM at beg and end of next row to mark armhole.
• Cont working in patt until piece measures 14 (15, 16, 17)" or approx 2½" shorter than desired length for girl's tunic; for boy's version, work 2 more rep of main patt st.

• **Work edge as foll:** Change to smaller needles and work 2 rep of edge patt st, then work rows 1–6 once more. For girl's tunic, back measures approximately 16½ (17½, 18½, 19½)"; for boy's shirttail, back measures approximately 18½ (19½, 20½, 21½)".
• BO all sts on next RS row with larger needle.

Front

- **Left shoulder:** With larger needles, CO 21 (22, 25, 26) sts. Knit 1 row.
- **Set-up row (WS):** K2 (5, 8, 11), PM, work in patt stitch of choice to end of row.
- Work in patt as est, working sts outside of marker in edge patt st. AT SAME TIME, inc 1 st at *beg* of each RS row for neck edge until you have 29 (31, 24, 36) sts. (Remember to work inc in patt st.) End after WS row. Place sts on holder.
- **Right shoulder:** CO 21 (22, 25, 26) sts.
- **Set-up row (WS):** K2 (5, 8, 11), PM, work in patt stitch of choice to end of row.
- Work in patt as est, working sts outside of marker in edge patt st. AT SAME TIME, inc 1 st at *end* of each RS row for neck edge until you have 29 (31, 34, 36) sts. (Remember to work inc in patt st.) End after WS row. You should be on same row of patt stitch as left shoulder. If you are not, knit extra rows needed to match up both sides on whichever shoulder is shy.
- Join pieces. Place both shoulders on needle with RS facing and inc edges in center. Work across left front, CO 10 (12, 12, 14) sts, work across right front: 68 (74, 80, 86) sts.
- Work as for back until piece measures 14 (15, 16, 17)" or approx 2½" shorter than desired length. Remember: front is 2" shorter than back for shirttail version.
- **Work edge:** Change to smaller needles and work 2 rep of edge patt st, then work rows 1–6 once more. For either version, front measures approximately 16½ (17½, 18½, 19½)".
- BO all sts on next RS row using larger needle.

Collar

- Sew right shoulder seam.
- With RS facing and smaller needles, PU 90 (94, 98, 102) sts evenly around neck and knit collar of your choice, as foll:

For a *rolled neck* (shown on girl's version), work back and forth in St st (knit on RS rows, purl on WS rows) until neck measures 1½". BO loosely using larger needle.

For a *hemmed crew neck* (shown on boy's version), work back and forth in K1, P1 ribbing until neck measures 1½". BO loosely using larger needle.

- Sew left shoulder seam and collar seam. Hem crew neck by folding collar to inside and loosely sewing BO edge to ridge where you picked up sts.

Sleeves

- With RS facing and larger needles, PU 66 (70, 70, 76) sts.
- **Set-up row:** K 7 (9, 9, 12), PM, work 52 sts in patt st of choice, PM, K 7 (9, 9, 12).
- Work even in patt as est, working sts outside of marker in edge patt st for 1 (1½, 1½, 2)".
- Cont working in patt st and AT SAME TIME, dec 1 st at beg and end of next and every 4th row until 34 (36, 38, 40) sts rem.
- Work even until sleeve measures 9 (10, 11, 12)" or is 2½" shorter than desired length. Change to smaller needles and work 2 rep of edge patt st. Work rows 1–6 once more.

Tip: If sleeve is desired length before you have decreased to correct number of stitches, work extra decreases evenly spaced across first right-side row of cuff.

- BO all sts using larger needle.

Finishing

- Sew side and sleeve seams. For shirttail version, remember that back is approximately 2" longer than front. Leave 1" open at bottom on both front and back for wearing ease.
- Block to measurements on diagram, opposite.
- Fold up sleeve cuffs if desired.

Care

These rugged garments require very little care. Wash them when you finish knitting and sewing them together to relax the yarn and make the sweaters softer and more comfortable. Machine wash and dry on gentle cycle with low heat.

Grow with Me

Most kids grow taller more quickly than they grow wider. So, if your child is getting too tall for his or her Take It from the Top sweater, you can easily add on to the body and sleeve length to get more wear out of the sweater. Because this sweater is knit from the top down, simply take out the bind-off row, attach more yarn, and add as many rows as desired before binding off again. Clever!

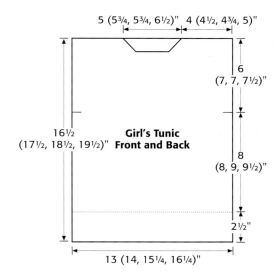

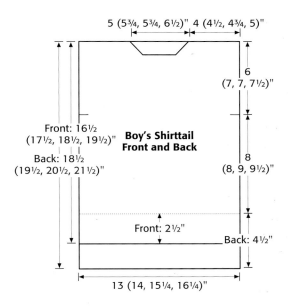

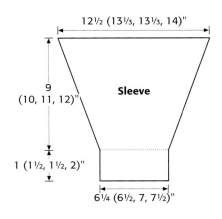

Garter-Check Rib Pattern

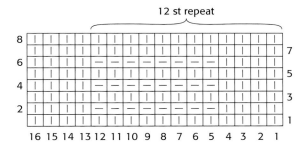

Garter-Check Cable Pattern

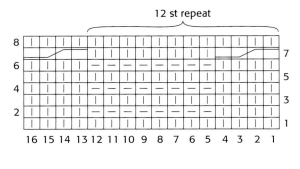

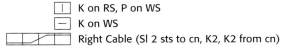

K on RS, P on WS
K on WS
Right Cable (Sl 2 sts to cn, K2, K2 from cn)

Welcome Baby Blanket

By Barbara Venishnick

Barbara wanted to create a piece that would suit either sex, and the sophisticated shades in the Spring Frost colorway fit that need. Rather than relying on worn-out standards such as yellow, mint, pink, and light blue, Spring Frost harmonizes watercolor shades of wisteria, silver, peach, and lichen to create a new twist for baby. Instead of a ruffle, the edging is actually a pleat with a bit of openwork, again making it suitable for both boys and girls.

This square blanket is quite versatile. Use it as a receiving blanket or lightweight carriage throw, or fold it in half diagonally and use it as a shawl for yourself! The merino is super soft against baby's skin and is fully machine washable and dryable. This breezy garment, knit from fingering-weight yarn, provides breathable warmth for the nippiest of climates.

The edging, which is knit first, is organized into rhythmic rows. Then, the circular construction of the blanket bends the rows into concentric boxes that form as you knit. This technique moves the various colors around in all directions, which prevents stacking or striping.

Vital Statistics

Skill Level: Intermediate
Finished Size: 33" square
Gauge: 20 sts and 40 rows = 4" in eyelet pattern stitch on US 6 needles

Materials

Yarn is by Cherry Tree Hill.

Yarn: 4 hanks of Supersock Merino (100% washable wool; 4 oz/370 yds) in colorway Spring Frost 🕷️**1**
Needles: US 6, 32" and 24" circular, and set of double-pointed, or size needed to obtain gauge
Notions: Safety pins or split-ring markers

Eyelet Pattern

Multiples of 2 sts, worked in the round

Rows 1, 3, and 5: Purl.
Rows 2, 4, 7, and 8: Knit.
Row 6: K1, *yo, K2tog; rep from * to end.

Blanket Instructions

The pleated ruffle is worked first back and forth on short needles, then the stitches for the center section are picked up and worked in the round, with the number of stitches decreased every other round.

Pleated Ruffle

- Using a pair of dpn, CO 15 sts.
- **Row 1 (WS):** K2, yo, K2tog, P8, M1 (inc 1 st by purling into front and back of next st), K2.
- **Row 2:** K16.
- **Row 3:** K2, yo, K2tog, P9, M1, K2.
- **Row 4 (short row):** K12, turn, P9, M1, K2.
- **Row 5:** K18.
- **Row 6:** K2, yo, K2tog, P1, (yo, P2tog) 5 times, P1, K2.
- **Row 7 (short row):** K13, turn, P9, P2tog, K2.
- **Row 8:** K17.
- **Row 9:** K2, yo, K2tog, P9, P2tog, K2.
- **Row 10:** K16.
- **Row 11:** K2, yo, K2tog, P8, P2tog, K2.
- **Row 12:** K15.
- **Row 13:** K2, yo, K2tog, K11.
- **Row 14 (short row):** K2, P8, turn, K10.
- **Row 15:** Rep row 14.
- **Row 16:** K2, P9, K4.
- Work rows 1–16 a total of 60 times, marking the center of the 1st, 16th, 31st, and 46th reps with safety pins or split-ring markers. BO 15 sts.

This soft and drapey baby blanket is knit with Supersock Merino in colorway Spring Frost.

The rhythm of the repeat is easy to master as you knit the outside edging first, then work toward the interior of the blanket.

Blanket Center

• Holding ruffle with RS facing and with longer circular needles, beg at *center* of first rep and PU 3 sts evenly spaced along top edge of second half of first ruffle. PU 136 sts evenly spaced across top to next 14 rep of ruffle; PU 2 sts evenly spaced across top of first half of 16th ruffle, PM, PU 3 sts across second half of 16th ruffle; PU 136 sts across next 14 rep of ruffle; PU 2 sts across first half of 31st ruffle, PM, PU 3 sts across top of second half of 31st ruffle; PU 136 sts across top of next 14 rep of ruffle, PU 2 sts across top of first half of 46th ruffle, PM, PU 3 sts across top of second half of 46th ruffle; PU 136 sts across last 14 rep of ruffle, PU 2 sts along top edge of first ruffle, and PM for beg of rnd: 564 total sts. Join.

• **First rnd (worked even):** *P1, sl 2 wyib, work row 1 of eyelet patt to within 2 sts of next marker, sl 2 wyib; rep from * 3 more times.

Note: A garter stitch is created between slipped knit stitches at each corner. As needed, change to smaller circular needles and then to double-pointed needles. At that point, place one side of square (stitches between markers) on each needle.

• When there are no sts left between corner garter sts and there are 5 sts on each needle, work as foll: (K2tog, K3) 4 times: 4 sts rem on each needle.
• Sl last st on 4th needle from right to left needle, then K2tog (first st of next rnd with last st of last rd), cont to K2tog all around: 8 sts rem.
• **Last rnd:** K2tog around. Cut yarn and draw through 4 rem sts.

Finishing

• Weave in ends on back side.
• Sew CO edge of ruffle to BO edge.
• Block gently, stretching slipped knit sts at each corner.

Care

Machine wash with mild detergent on delicate cycle and dry on low heat.

• **Dec rnd:** *K2, SSK, work row 2 of eyelet patt to within 3 sts of next marker, K2tog, K1; rep from * 3 more times.
• Cont alternating even and dec rows and AT SAME TIME work all 8 rows of eyelet patt in order.

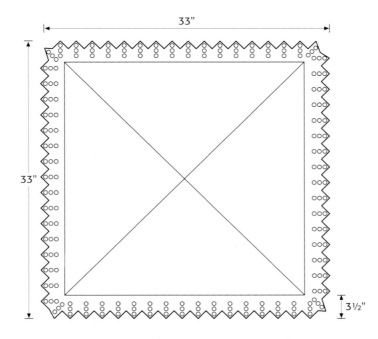

Knitting with Textured Yarns

TEXTURED, hand-painted yarns come in many kinds of fibers and gauges, from the thinnest nylon eyelash, to brushed animal fibers such as mohair, to the chunkiest cotton chenille. Giving texture and color equal emphasis has become increasingly popular, especially in whimsical garments for children. The advantages are numerous, as texture adds interest to plain knitting, such as stockinette stitch, and in painted yarns, the texture moves color along and tends to break up striping or stacking. Many designers opt for textured yarn in place of a complex pattern stitch. It makes a garment easier to knit and lets the yarn do the work. Emphasizing both texture and color can result in a more complex-looking garment with the appeal of wearable art.

Disadvantages of knitting with textured yarns can be numerous as well. Beginning knitters often find even the gauge swatch daunting, because it may be difficult to maintain an even tension, and gauge is often tough to determine. Rather than harmonizing, the texture and colors can fight with one another and obscure pattern stitches. Prudent knitters will decide which to feature at the outset—texture or color—and decide on a simple pattern stitch or none at all, depending upon the extent of the texture. To make the most of the yarn's texture, my advice is to keep the knitting simple, as we've done with the projects in this section.

Snuggle Throws

By Holly Rodriguez

Designer Holly Rodriguez was in the mood for a quick-knit project with textured yarn. All-cotton Plush fit the bill, because it's fast and easy to knit. It's also machine washable and dryable. The cuddly texture of the yarn gives depth to a simple stockinette stitch and feels pleasantly warm and soft on the lap as the needles click away. This child-size afghan was so quick to knit that Holly decided to make a baby blanket, too!

A child of any age would love to snuggle up with this lightweight blanket. The bright blues and greens and subtle grays of the Green Mountain Madness colorway are suitable for either a boy's or a girl's room. For the baby blanket, Holly used the gender-neutral Spring Frost colorway.

This blanket is a great introduction to knitting with oversized, textured yarn because it's simple to knit, requiring only a stockinette stitch bordered by an even easier garter stitch. Large needles make quick work of the chunky yarn. Keep the stitches loose on the needle and your knitting will flow at a fast rate.

Vital Statistics

Finished Size: approximately 30" x 35" blanket (42" x 45" afghan)
Gauge: 7 sts = 4" in stockinette stitch on US 15 needles

Materials

All yarns are by Cherry Tree Hill.

Yarn: 2 (3) hanks of Plush (100% preshrunk cotton chenille; 8 oz/185 yds) in colorway Spring Frost (Green Mountain Madness) **6**
Needles: US 15, 24" circular needles, or size needed to obtain gauge

Blanket Instructions

• Loosely CO 54 (76) sts. Knit 6 rows for garter st border.
• **Row 1:** Knit.
• **Row 2:** K3, purl to last 3 sts, K3.
• Rep rows 1 and 2 until you have about 16 yds of yarn left, or enough to work 7 rows.
• Knit 6 rows. BO all sts loosely.
• Weave in all ends.

Care

Machine wash, tumble dry.

The child's afghan is shown in colorway Green Mountain Madness; the smaller throw for baby (page 49) is shown in colorway Spring Frost.

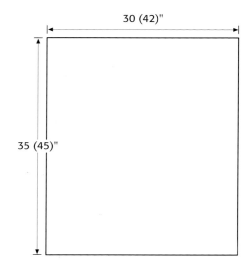

30 (42)"

35 (45)"

Zebra Tunic

By JoAnne Turcotte

This novel project grew from a collaboration between JoAnne and me. We wanted to create a simple vest that would both grow with the child and also show a fancy textured yarn to its best advantage. This tunic top is knit all in one piece, up the front and over the top, with no shoulder seams or side sewing. A variation of the three-needle bind off is used to attach the front pocket. The sides are secured with sturdy crocheted ties. Loosen the ties as your child grows, and see this garment worn again and again.

An over-the-head tunic is simple to put on—even for toddlers, who are just learning to dress themselves. When working single crochet around the neck edge, remember to maintain the overall circumference of the neck opening. Toddlers have large heads in comparison to their bodies, so the head opening needs to be oversized.

The colorway Old Rose carries the simple stitch pattern perfectly. Knitters will sense the presence of an old English rose garden, bringing thoughts of a cool spring day—the type of day that calls for just a light cover-up, such as this easy-wear tunic.

Vital Statistics

Skill Level: Easy
Children's Sizes: 12 months (2T, 3T)
Finished Chest Measurements: 26 (30, 33)"
(Size is approximate; the open sides allow room to grow.)
Finished Lengths: 12 (13, 14)"
Gauge: 14 sts = 4" in stockinette stitch on US 8 needles

Materials

Yarn is by Cherry Tree Hill.

Yarn: 2 (2, 2) hanks of Zebra Caribe (rayon, cotton, polyseed blend; 8 oz/270 yds) in colorway Old Rose 5
Needles: US 7 and US 8, or size needed to obtain gauge, and a spare size 7 needle
Notions: Stitch markers, size J crochet hook, tapestry needle

Garter Stitch

Knit all rows.

The yarn in this photo is fancy Zebra Caribe before and after hand painting. Dyed in a bold colorway, Zebra transforms this simple vest into a piece of wearable art.

Stockinette Stitch

Knit all RS rows; purl all WS rows.

Tunic Instructions

Make pocket first, as you'll need to attach it to the front of the tunic as you knit.

Tunic shown in colorway Old Rose, size 12 months.

Pocket

- With smaller needles, loosely CO 24 (26, 28) sts. Work in garter st until total length is 5", ending with WS row.
- Cut yarn and leave sts on spare size 7 needle (referred to as "pocket needle").

Tunic

- With smaller needles, loosely CO 42 (48, 54) sts. Work in garter st for 6 rows. Change to larger needles.
- **Row 1 (RS):** Knit.
- **Row 2 (WS):** K4, purl to last 4 sts, K4.
- **Row 3:** K4, inc 1 by knitting into front and back of next st, knit to last 5 sts, inc 1 in next st, K4.
- **Row 4:** K4, purl to last 4 sts, K4.

- Rep last 4 rows once more: 46 (52, 58) total sts. PM at side edge.
- Work even in St st, working 4 sts on each edge in garter st, until total length is 5½", ending with WS row.
- **Attach pocket:** Work across 11 (13, 15) sts. Holding 24 (26, 28) sts on pocket needle parallel in front of tunic sts, work next 24 (26, 28) sts of tunic tog with sts from pocket needle. (Knit sts tog as you would in 3-needle BO, but don't BO). Work across rest of row in patt.
- Cont working in patt until total length is 10 (11, 12)", ending with WS row.
- **Shape neck:** Work across 16 (19, 21) sts. Turn, leaving rest of sts unworked on needle, and work back across row. Next row: Work to last 3 sts, K2tog, K1. Work back. Rep last 2 rows twice more: 13 (16, 18) sts. Work even until total length

is 12 (13, 14)", ending with RS row. PM at side edge to indicate shoulder. Place these 13 (16, 18) shoulder sts on spare needle.
• Reattach yarn at center neck edge. BO next 14 (14, 16) sts. Work to end of row: 16 (19, 21) sts. Work back across row.
• **Next row:** K1, SSK, work to end of row. Work back.
• Rep last 2 rows twice more: 13 (16, 18) sts.
• Work even until total length is 12 (13, 14)", ending with RS row.
• **CO row (WS):** Work across shoulder sts, loosely CO 20 (20, 22) sts, and then work across shoulder sts from spare needle: 46 (52, 58) total sts. Work even until total length from shoulder marker is same as length from front side-edge marker to shoulder marker, ending with WS row.
• Beg dec as foll:
>   **Row 1:** K4, K2tog, knit to last 6 sts, SSK, K4.
>   **Row 2:** K4, purl to last 4 sts, K4.
>   **Row 3:** Knit.
>   **Row 4:** K4, purl to last 4 sts, K4.
>   Rep last 4 rows once more: 42 (48, 54) sts.
• Work 6 rows of garter st. BO all sts loosely.

Finishing

• Sew bottom of pocket to tunic, just above garter-st bottom border of tunic front.
• With RS facing and using crochet hook, loosely work 1 row of sc around neck edge, making sure to keep finished neck opening big enough for toddler's head.
• Make 4 crochet chains, each 8" long. Attach to side edges—1 on each side, front and back, about 5" below shoulder. Tie in bows on sides.

Care

Block very lightly with a steam iron. Hand or machine wash and either tumble dry or lay flat to dry.

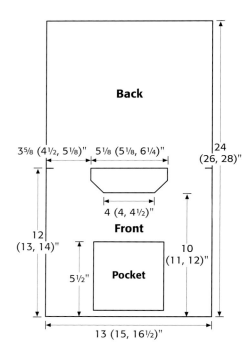

Love-Leaf Vest

By Judy Sumner

When designing this vest, Judy Sumner knew she wanted to include something from nature in it. She incorporated a whimsical stem with two leaves to form a simple join, adding a designer touch to an otherwise plain hook-and-eye closure. Children will love opening and closing the vest by themselves. There are no buttons to struggle with, only the little hook-and-eye fastener to link the leaves. The cool cotton is lightweight and unbelievably soft.

The vest is designed in one piece so that there are no bulky seams to deal with—an advantage for thick chenille and other bulky-weight yarns. Even the shoulders are unseamed; instead, they're easily grafted with kitchener stitch. The leaves are knit separately and then appliquéd over the stockinette fabric. A bit of garter stitch along the vest edges keeps them from curling.

Life's a Beach is a carefree color combination of clear sun yellow punctuated by sky turquoise and grass green. The bright shades bring to mind simple childhood days and the sheer joy of a bright summer. When cooler weather comes, this cheerful vest will be a reminder of the warm summer sun.

Vital Statistics

Skill Level: Easy
Children's Sizes: Small (Medium, Large)
Finished Chest Measurements: 28 (30, 32)"
Finished Lengths: 14 (15, 16)"
Gauge: 2 sts and 3 rows = 1" in stockinette stitch on US 10 needles

Materials

Yarn is by Cherry Tree Hill.

Yarn: 1 (2, 2) hanks of Plush (100% preshrunk cotton chenille; 8 oz/185 yds) in colorway Life's a Beach (6)
Needles: US 10, 29" circular and set of double-pointed, or size needed to obtain gauge
Notions: 4 stitch holders, 1 large-eye tapestry needle, 1 hook-and-eye set, matching thread

Vest Instructions

Work the body in one piece to armholes.
• With circular needles, CO 56 (60, 64) sts.
• **Row 1 (RS):** Knit.
• **Row 2:** K2, purl to last 2 sts, K2.
• Work these 2 rows until piece measures 7½ (8, 8)" from beg, ending with WS row.

• **Next row:** K 13 (14, 15) sts. BO 2 sts. K 26 (28, 30) sts. Place rem sts on holder for left front.
• Turn work. K2, purl to 2 sts before BO, K2. Place rem sts on holder for right front. Turn work and knit all rem sts for vest back.
• Cont to work back in St st patt (first 2 and last 2 sts in garter st) until armholes measure 6½ (7, 8)", ending with a WS row.
• On next row, K 6 (7, 8), K2tog, BO center 10 sts, K2tog, knit rem sts, and place shoulder sts on holders. Leave yarn tails long enough (about 20") to join shoulders.

Left Front

• With RS facing, attach yarn at armhole edge on left front. BO 2 sts and knit rem 13 (14, 15) sts. Turn work. K2, purl to last 2 sts, K2.
• **Shape neck:** Cont in est patt, dec sts either after K2 border on RS (K2tog) or before K2 border on WS of work (P2tog). Work foll number of dec:
    Small: Dec every 2nd row 2 times and then every 3rd row 4 times.
    Medium: Dec every 3rd row 6 times.
    Large: Dec every 3rd row 2 times and then every 4th row 4 times.
• Work even until front is same length as back. Put sts on holder.

Vest shown in Plush chenille in colorway Life's a Beach, size Small. The simple stockinette pattern allows the high-contrast colorway to do the work.

Right Front

- **Row 1:** With WS facing, K2, purl to last 2 sts, K2.
- **Row 2 (RS):** Knit across.
- Work these 2 rows, dec as for left front.
- When right front is same length as back, end with WS row and place sts on holder.

Plain Leaf

- Using dpn, CO 3 sts.
- **Row 1:** P3.
- **Row 2:** K1, yo, K1, yo, K1.
- **Row 3:** P5.
- **Row 4:** K2, yo, K1, yo, K2.
- **Row 5:** P7.

- **Row 6:** Sl 1, K1, psso, K3, K2tog.
- **Row 7:** P5.
- **Row 8:** Sl 1, K1, psso, K1, K2tog.
- **Row 9:** P3.
- **Row 10:** Sl 1, K2tog, psso. Fasten off (BO and pull yarn tail through last st to prevent unraveling).

Leaf with Stem

Detail shown as inset above.

- Using dpn, CO 2 sts.
- Work in 2-st I-cord (see page 108 for instructions) for 3" to make stem.
- On last row, inc 1 in first st, K1: 3 sts total.
- Cont leaf as before. Fasten off.

Finishing

• With sts from back shoulder on 1 dpn and sts from front shoulder on another needle, graft sts using kitchener st (see page 108). This will eliminate a bulky seam at the shoulders.
• Pin leaves on front of garment, corresponding to where you'll place hook and eye on underside, then tack them down with matching thread.
• On back side, sew hook and eye in place with matching thread, and leaves will appear to join in front when vest is fastened.

Care

Hand wash and lay flat to dry.

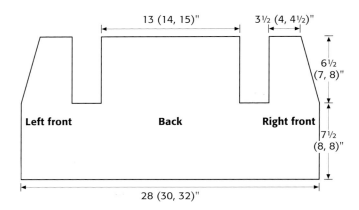

Garden Party

By Terri Shea

Summer weddings, garden parties, and other get-togethers are perfect opportunities for little girls to wear something special. A textured novelty yarn like Mélange can jazz up the simplest style. This pullover is worked in a stockinette stitch with a tiny garter-stitch hem to prevent rolling. The ruffled sleeve edge, worked with easy decreases, adds a fun detail that little girls will love.

This pullover features a shallow V-neck, buttoned shoulder opening, and deep armholes, making it easy to put on. The sleeves are designed to be a little short to keep busy hands free to explore and play. They're also fashioned wide, so if your child grows quickly, the sweater can be worn with ¾-length sleeves and continue to look good.

The bright colors of the Champlain Sunset colorway appeal to active little girls. A more romantic look could be achieved with softer colors, such as Gypsy Rose or Spring Frost. Multistrand yarns like Mélange can split when knit with sharp-tipped or "sticky" needles (ones that really grip the yarn), so I recommend blunt-tipped, aluminum needles. In addition, bulky or novelty yarn is not good for seaming, so use pearl cotton or a smooth, finer-gauge cotton yarn in a matching color for assembling the garment.

Vital Statistics

Skill Level: Easy
Children's Sizes: 2 (4, 6, 8)
Finished Chest Measurements: 24½ (26½, 28½, 31½)"
Gauge: 16 sts and 23 rows = 4" in stockinette stitch on US 8 needles

Materials

Yarn is by Cherry Tree Hill.

Yarn: 2 (2, 3, 3) hanks of Mélange (78% rayon, 12% cotton novelty blend, 10% cotton chenille; 8 oz/308 yds) in colorway Champlain Sunset (4)
Needles: US 8 or size needed to obtain gauge
Notions: Safety pin, pearl cotton or smooth cotton yarn for seaming, medium-size crochet hook, 1½" diameter button (optional), tapestry needle

Stockinette Stitch

Knit all RS rows; purl all WS rows.

Sweater Instructions

The front, back, and sleeves are all worked separately and then sewn together.

Back

- CO 49 (53, 57, 63) sts.
- Knit 3 rows to form a garter-st edge.
- Switch to St st and work until piece measures 8 (9, 12, 13)", ending on WS row.
- Shape armholes:
    Row 1 (RS): K2, K2tog, knit to last 4 sts, SSK, K2.
    Row 2: Purl.
    Work these 2 rows 5 (6, 6, 7) times total: 39 (41, 45, 49) sts rem.
- Work even until armhole measures 6 (6½, 7, 7½)". BO all sts.

Front

- Work as for back through armhole shaping, ending on WS row.
- **Next row (RS):** Work across 19 (20, 22, 24) sts. Place center st on safety pin. Join second ball and work rest of row, then purl right shoulder sts on next WS row.

Sweater shown in colorway Champlain Sunset, size 2.

- Shape right shoulder:

    Row 1 (RS): K2, K2tog, knit to end.

    Row 2: Purl.

    Work these 2 rows 9 (10, 10, 11) times: 10 (10, 12, 13) shoulder sts rem.

- Work even until same length as back. BO rem shoulder sts.
- **Shape left shoulder:** Return to first ball attached to left shoulder. Purl WS row, then beg shaping:

    Row 1 (RS): K2, SSK, knit to end.

    Row 2: Purl.

    Work these 2 rows 9 (10, 10, 11) times: 10 (10, 12, 13) shoulder sts rem.

- Work even until same length as back. BO rem shoulder sts, leaving about 10" tail for button loop.

Sleeves (Make 2)

- Loosely CO 114 (114, 122, 122) sts.
- **Rows 1, 3, and 5 (WS):** Purl all sts.
- **Rows 2 and 4:** K1, K2tog to last st, K1.
- These 5 rows complete ruffle: 30 (30, 32, 32) sts rem.
- Work rest of sleeve in St st, inc at beg and end of row every 4 rows 5 (0, 0, 4) times, every 5 rows 5 (10, 5, 0) times, and every 6 rows 0 (0, 5, 8) times: 50 (50, 52, 56) sts rem.
- Work even until sleeve measures 9 (10, 11¼, 12¼)" excluding ruffle, ending on WS row.
- Shape cap:

    Row 1 (RS): K2, K2tog, knit to last 4 sts, SSK, K2.

    Row 2: Purl all sts.

    Work these 2 rows 6 (6, 6, 7) times total: 38 (38, 40, 42) sts rem. BO all sts.

Finishing

• Block all pieces to measurements given in illustration below (no need to pin ruffle for blocking).

• Sew shoulder seams with pearl cotton or smooth cotton yarn. **Optional shoulder button:** On left shoulder, beg at sleeve edge and stitch seam for ½" only. Pin shoulder, if necessary, to complete finishing.

• Sew in sleeves. Sew underarm sleeve seams and side seams.

• Weave in ends.

• **Neckband:** Beg at left shoulder and with RS facing, PU 12 (12, 14, 14) sts along left front, knit center front st from safety pin, PU 12 (12, 14, 14) sts along right front, and 19 (21, 21, 23) sts along back neck. Turn and BO all sts.

• **Shoulder button loops:** With tail at left shoulder, use crochet hook and chain 4 sts, then pull through selvage and weave in end. Sew button at left shoulder.

Care

Hand wash in cool water and dry flat.

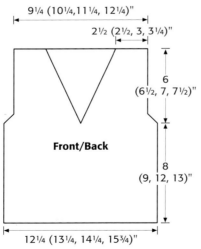

9¼ (10¼, 11¼, 12¼)"

2½ (2½, 3, 3¼)"

Front/Back

6 (6½, 7, 7½)"

8 (9, 12, 13)"

12¼ (13¼, 14¼, 15¾)"

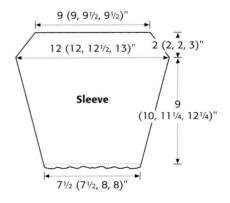

9 (9, 9½, 9½)"

12 (12, 12½, 13)"

2 (2, 2, 3)"

Sleeve

9 (10, 11¼, 12¼)"

7½ (7½, 8, 8)"

Beachcomber

By Terri Shea

For designer Terri Shea, this sweater recalls the small coastal town of Seaside, Oregon, which is remarkable for its rocky beaches, promenade, and holiday-at-the-shore atmosphere. Because "beach weather" on the Oregon coast can mean wet and gray, warm sweaters are necessary year-round in Seaside.

This unisex pullover features a big pocket perfect for collecting rocks, shells, and other beach treasures. It also has a buttoned shoulder, making it easy to get on and off. The soft cotton yarn is cozy and breathable, ensuring that the sweater will be worn again and again. The design is worked flat in an allover pattern, a modified chevron stitch. Setting in a pocket is much easier to do than it is to describe, so don't be intimidated. You simply knit the pocket first, and then knit it in where called for in the instructions.

The pinks, purples, and dusky indigo of the Winterberry colorway make this pullover easy for any little girl to pair with jeans or denim shorts. In addition, the subtle colors don't compete with the textured yarn and stitch details. To give this garment a boyish flair, try it with another low-contrast colorway, such as Green Mountain Madness or Java.

Vital Statistics

Skill Level: Intermediate
Children's Sizes: Small (18 months) [Medium (2T), Large (3T), X-Large (4T)]
Finished Chest Sizes: 25 (26½, 28, 29½)"
Finished Lengths: 13 (14, 15, 16)"
Gauge: 22 sts and 26 rows = 4" in stockinette waves pattern on US 6 needles

Materials

Yarn is by Cherry Tree Hill.

Yarn: 2 (3, 3, 4) hanks of Cotton Bouclé (100% cotton; 4 oz/170 yds) in colorway Winterberry (**3**)
Needles: US 6 straight, double-pointed, or 16" circular, or size needed to obtain gauge, and US 4 double-pointed or 16" circular
Notions: Stitch holder; safety pins; 3 buttons, ½" diameter; 1 button, 1" diameter; tapestry needle

Garter Waves

Multiple of 11 sts

Row 1 (WS): Knit.
Row 2: *K2tog, K3, M1, K1, M1, K3, SSK; rep from * to end.
Rep rows 1 and 2 for patt.

Stockinette Waves

Multiple of 11 sts

Row 1 (WS): Purl.
Row 2: *K2tog, K3, M1, K1, M1, K3, SSK; rep from * to end.
Rep rows 1 and 2 for patt.

Sweater Instructions

Pullover is worked flat. Pattern is worked inside selvage stitches (a knit stitch at each end on both right and wrong sides), which are included in the instructions. When measuring length, measure from the top of a zigzag, following the knit stitch between the increases as a guide.

Sweater is shown in colorway Winterberry, size 3T.

Pocket

• With larger needles, CO 33 sts (all sizes) and work in stockinette waves patt for 28 rows or until piece measures 5½", ending with WS row.
• Place sts on holder and set aside.

Back

• With larger needles, CO 69 (73, 77, 81) sts.
• **Row 1 (WS):** Knit.
• **Row 2:** Est garter waves patt according to size:
  Small: K2, M1, K3, SSK, *K2tog, K3, M1, K1, M1, K3, SSK; rep from * to last 7 sts, K2tog, K3, M1, K2.
  Medium: K1, K2tog, K1, M1, K1, M1, K2, SSK, *K2tog, K3, M1, K1, M1, K3, SSK; rep from * to last 9 sts, K2tog, K2, M1, K1, M1,

K1, SSK, K1.
  Large: K1, K2tog, K2, M1, K1, M1, K3, SSK, *K2tog, K3, M1, K1, M1, K3, SSK; rep from * to last 11 sts, K2tog, K3, M1, K1, M1, K2, SSK, K1.
  X-Large: K2, *K2tog, K3, M1, K1, M1, K3, SSK; rep from * to last 2 sts, K2.
• Work in garter waves patt for 6 ridges, then work in St waves patt until piece measures 7½ (8, 8½, 9½)" from CO edge.
• **Shape armhole:** BO 4 sts at beg of next 2 rows: 61 (65, 69, 73) sts rem. Cont in patt, making sure to K1 selvage st on each edge, until piece measures 12½ (13½, 14½, 15½)" from CO edge.
• **Shape back neck:** On next row, work 20 (22, 24, 25) sts, BO center 21 (21, 21, 23) sts, attach another ball of yarn and work across rem 20 (22,

65

24, 25) sts to complete row. Working both sides at once, dec 1 st at each side of neck opening. Work 1 row even. Repeat dec row 0 (0, 1, 1) more time(s). Cont even in patt until piece measures 13 (14, 15, 16)". BO 19 (21, 22, 23) sts across right shoulder, work left shoulder an additional 6 rows and BO.

Front

- Work as for back to armholes.
- **Next row:** BO 4 sts to shape armhole. Work in patt for 14 (16, 18, 20) sts, place center 33 sts onto holder. Slip pocket sts from holder onto left needle so same side of work as sweater is facing you. Work across pocket sts and then complete row in patt. Turn, BO 4 sts, work to end of row.
- Cont working as for back until piece measures 11 (12, 13, 14)". Pocket will be knit into body of work. It will hang loose on WS of sweater front. (You may want to safety pin the pocket opening closed if it annoys you as you work.)
- **Shape front neck:** Work across 23 (25, 26, 27) sts, place center 15 (15, 17, 19) sts on holder, attach another ball of yarn, and work remaining 23 (25, 26, 27) sts to complete row. Working both sides at once, dec 1 st at each neck edge EOR 4 times. Cont working right shoulder in patt until piece measures 13 (14, 15, 16)". BO 19 (21, 23, 24) sts across right shoulder.
- Work left shoulder sts even in patt until piece measures 12½ (13½, 15, 15½)". Continue to work these sts in garter st.
- **Row 1 (RS):** K 5 (6, 7, 7), K2tog, yo, K 5 (6, 7, 7), K2tog, yo, K 5 (5, 5, 6); 2 buttonholes made.
- **Row 2:** Knit.
- BO in purl.

Sleeves (Make 2)

- With larger needles, CO 33 (33, 35, 35) sts.
- **Row 1 (WS):** Knit.
- **Row 2:** Est garter waves patt according to size:
  Small and Medium: K1, K2tog, K2, M1, K1, M1, K3, SSK, K2tog, K3, M1, K1, M1, K3, SSK, K2tog, K2, M1, K1, M1, K3, SSK, K1.

  Large and X-Large: K1, *K2tog, K3, M1, K1, M1, K3, SSK; rep from * to last st, K1.
- Work 3 (3, 4, 4) ridges of garter waves, then switch to St waves patt.
- **Begin sleeve shaping as foll:** inc each side of row every 3 rows 2 (12, 4, 2) times; every 4 rows 7 (0, 9, 12) times: 51 (57, 61, 63) sts rem.
- Cont in patt until sleeve measures 7 (8, 10, 11)". BO all sts.

Note: When working the shaping simultaneously, remember to always work the decreases and increases in pairs to keep the chevron pattern going. If you don't have enough stitches on the needles to do both a decrease and an increase, simply work in St st until you have enough stitches to do the increase-decrease pair.

Finishing

- **Pocket:**
  Beg with RS facing, work 3 rows garter waves patt on the 33 sts on holder on front of garment.
  Row 4: Work in patt across 15 sts, BO center 3 sts, and complete row in patt.
  Row 5: Work in patt across 15 sts, CO 3 sts, and complete row in patt.
  Rows 6 and 7: Work in patt.
  Row 8 (WS): BO in knit.

- Sew pocket trim in place on RS of sweater; sew pocket sides and bottom in place on WS of sweater.
- Sew right shoulder. Use safety pins to pin left shoulder closed, with front overlapping back.
- Sew in sleeves. Sew underarm sleeve seams and side seams, leaving garter-waves trim open if desired.
- **Rolled neck:** With smaller 16" circular needles or dpn and RS facing, beg a left shoulder and PU 58 (58, 62, 66) sts around neck edge. Work back and forth as follows:

> **Row 1 (WS):** Purl.
> **Row 2 (RS):** K2, SSK, yo, knit to end: buttonhole made.
> Work 3 rows in St st.
> BO all sts in knit.

- Attach buttons to shoulder back and pocket.
- Weave in ends and block with steam.

Care

Hand wash and lay flat to dry, or if using washable buttons, machine wash and tumble dry on low.

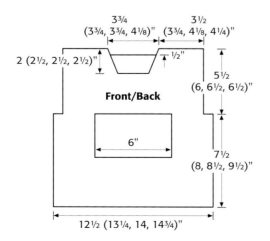

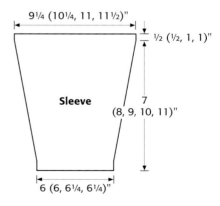

Knitting with Novelty Yarns

KNITTING with novelty yarns (or "novelties" for short) takes the concept of knitting with those textured yarns discussed in the previous chapter even further. Some novelties are not yarns at all, but strips of fabric, beaded elastic, lengths of ladder-chain lace—the list goes on! By pairing different sizes and shapes of the widest range of fibers imaginable with hand-dyed colorways, knitters have found that they can achieve almost any effect.

Advantages far outnumber disadvantages when working with novelties. By definition, novelty yarns are new and unusual. They add a designer touch to the simplest of garments and freshen up classic patterns. Although novelties tend to be expensive, a little can go a long way. As trim, such as fake-fur cuffs or glitter edgings, novelty yarns enhance plainer garments, adding a whimsical quality. Most often, novelties are knit with little or no pattern stitch, letting the yarn shine. This is wonderful for beginner knitters who crave that designer edge. And children love the special touches. Garments made of novelty yarns are fun to knit and fun to wear!

Common disadvantages center on what I call the intimidation factor. Many knitters are unfamiliar with yarns containing ribbon, glitter, or eyelash spinning off central cores or plied with other yarns to form a blend. These yarns can be slippery, split easily, and defy gauge. Another potential problem is that novelties are often discontinued faster than regular yarns because of their faddish nature. So, it is very important to purchase enough novelty yarn in the color needed at the outset, and that may be difficult too, as it is often impossible to visualize what the yarn will look like knit.

The next set of projects introduce knitters to easily accessible novelties and range from beginner to intermediate in scope. I think that you will find them as much fun to knit as we did!

Fun-Fur Hat and Mitts

By Donna Druchunas

Faux fur is fashionable on all kinds of garments, especially as trim, so it is no surprise that a version should find its way to projects for kids. The garter-stitch fabric is quick to knit and is so stretchy that it will be almost impossible to outgrow these mitts and this cap. For tiny tots, fold up the brim of the hat. When a child gets bigger, you can fold it down.

The cuffs of these mitts and the brim of the hat are worked with large needles and two strands of yarn held together. The main sections are worked with a single strand of wool yarn and smaller needles. To compensate for the different gauges, you'll simply increase stitches in the first row of knitting with the single yarn by knitting into each strand of yarn as if it were a separate stitch, as indicated in the pattern instructions.

Fun Fur is nothing more than glitter nylon eyelash on a sturdy core. It can be knit singly, as a runner stranded with other yarns, or doubled to create a furrier effect. With this novelty yarn, you can make your own knitted fur using just a garter stitch!

Vital Statistics

Skill Level: Easy
Mitts: Children's Sizes: 4–6 (8–10)
Finished Lengths: 6½ (8)"
Cap: One size fits all
Gauge: 5 sts = 1" in garter stitch on US 6 needles

Materials

All yarns are by Cherry Tree Hill.

Yarns:
Color A—1 hank of Superwash Merino DK (100% Superwash merino; 4 oz/280 yds) in colorway Quarry Hill ③
Color B—1 hank of Fun Fur (100% nylon; 50 g/135 yds) in colorway Quarry Hill
Needles: US 6, or size needed to obtain gauge, and US 9
Notions: Scrap yarn, stitch markers, pom-pom maker, tapestry needle

Garter Stitch

Knit all rows.

For a different effect, try a multicolored yarn with a solid Fun Fur.

Cap Instructions

The cap is shown knit with both yarns in the same colorway. For more contrast, choose a solid color Fun Fur such as Black or Cherry.

Brim

• Using larger needles and 1 strand each of A and B held tog, CO 60 sts.
• Work in garter st for 2".

Crown

• Switch to smaller needles and work inc row: Using 1 strand of A only, *K2, knit into each strand of next st separately; rep from * to end: 80 sts.
• Cont with 1 strand of A, work even in garter st until cap measures 6" from CO edge.
• **Dec row 1:** *K2, K2tog; rep from * to end: 60 sts.

Hatt and mitts are shown in Superwash Merino DK and Fun Fur, both in colorway Quarry Hill, size 8–10.

- Work 5 rows even.
- **Dec row 2:** *K2, K2tog; rep from * to end: 45 sts.
- Work 5 rows even.
- **Dec row 3:** *K1, K2tog; rep from * to end: 30 sts.
- Work 3 rows even.
- **Dec row 4:** K2tog across: 15 sts.
- Work 1 row even.
- **Dec row 5:** K2tog across to last st, K1: 8 sts.
- Break yarn, leaving 10" tail. With tapestry needle, thread tail through remaining 8 sts and pull firmly to close. Fasten off.

Finishing

- Sew back seam and weave in ends.
- Make pom-pom with Fun Fur, referring to page 109 for instructions. Attach pom-pom to top of hat.

Mitts Instructions

Make one left and one right mitten.

Left Mitt

- Using larger needles and 1 strand each of A and B held tog, CO 21 (24) sts.
- Work in garter st for 2".
- Switch to smaller needles and work inc row: Using 1 strand of A only, *K2, knit into each strand of next st separately; rep from * to end: 28 (32) sts.
- Work even until mitt measures 3½ (4)" from CO edge.

- **Make thumb hole:** K 14 (16). Using scrap yarn, K 6 (7). Slip scrap yarn sts back to left needle and reknit 6 (7) thumb-hole sts with working yarn. Knit to end of row.
- Cont to work even until mitt measures 5 (6)" from CO edge.
- On next WS row, K 14 (16), PM, K 14 (16).
- **Shape top:** Dec on next row and every 4 rows: K1, K2tog, knit to last 3 sts before marker, K2tog, K1, sl marker, K1, K2tog, knit to last 3 sts, K2tog, K1.
- When less than 10 sts rem, break yarn, leaving 6" tail. With tapestry needle, thread tail through rem sts and pull firmly to close. Fasten off.
- **Thumb:** With RS facing, carefully remove waste yarn and sl sts onto 2 needles. You should have 5 (6) sts on the needle above the thumb opening and 6 (7) sts on the needle below the opening.
- Join yarn and knit across sts from both needles, PU 1 st in gap between st from top and bottom of thumb.
- Slip all sts onto 1 needle and work in garter st for 1½ (2)" or until thumb is just shy of desired length.
- **Next row:** K2tog to end of row. Break yarn, leaving 6" tail. With tapestry needle, thread tail through rem sts and pull firmly to close. Fasten off.

Right Mitt

Work as for left mitt except for thumb placement: K 8 (9), K 6 (7) sts with scrap yarn. Sl scrap yarn sts back to left needle and reknit 7 sts with working yarn. Knit to end of row.

Finishing

- Sew side seam and thumb seam on both mittens.
- Weave in ends.
- No blocking is needed for any of these items.

Care

Hand wash. Lay flat to dry.

Plush Hat and Muff

By Terri Shea

Classic designs never go out of style. The idea for this accessory duo came from vintage fashion-magazine illustrations. We wanted the look of a fur muff without the heaviness or excessive warmth. The cotton chenille and faux fur weigh in at just a few ounces and provide a fun addition to any little girl's wardrobe. Because the fur yarn can be too tickly for some children's faces, the hatband is sewn on top of the hat where it is merely decorative.

Choosing the Cabin Fever colorway for the Plush chenille yarn seemed like a natural choice for a wild-animal look. The black sparkle trim provides great contrast with the slate color in the Plush. The two yarns have quite different textures, and they also vary widely in gauge. To compensate, the Fun Fur is worked doubled. Overall gauge is not a big factor, however, since small hands will fit into a muff for years to come and the hat can be blocked to size. To shape the hat, mist it with water and then dry it over a mold, such as a small plate placed on top of a canister.

Vital Statistics

Skill Level (Hat): Easy
Skill Level (Muff): Beginner
Children's Size: One size fits most
Gauge: 10 sts and 16 rows = 4" in Plush on US 9 needles for hat
9 sts and 15 rows = 4" in Plush on US 11 needles for muff

Materials

All yarns are by Cherry Tree Hill.

Yarn:
Color A—1 hank of Plush (100% preshrunk cotton chenille; 8 oz /185 yds) in colorway Cabin Fever (6)
Color B—1 hank of Fun Fur (nylon with glitter; 50 g/135 yds) in Black (3)
Needles: US 9 straight and double-pointed, or size needed to obtain gauge, for hat; US 11, or size needed to obtain gauge, for muff
Notions: Stitch marker, tapestry needle

Stockinette Stitch

In the round: Knit all rows.
Back and forth: Knit all RS rows; purl all WS rows.

Hat Instructions

Note: When slipping stitches, always slip as if to purl, except for the SKP.
SKP: Sl 1 st as if to knit, sl next st as if to purl, insert left needle into sts from left to right and knit the 2 sts tog.

• Using A and dpn, CO 50 sts. Divide sts onto 3 needles and join, making certain not to twist sts. Mark beg of rnd.
• Knit all rnds until piece measures 2".
• **Next rnd:** Inc as foll: M1, K16, M1, K17, M1, K17: 53 sts.
• Knit 5 rnds even.
• **Next rnd:** Inc as foll: K9, M1, K17, M1, K18, M1, K9: 56 sts.
• Purl next 3 rnds, dec 2 sts evenly on third rnd: 54 sts rem.
• Work crown as foll:
   Rnd 1: *K7, SKP; rep from * around.
   Rnd 2: Knit.
   Rnd 3: *K6, SKP; rep from * around.
   Rnd 4: Knit.
   Rnd 5: *K5, SKP; rep from * around.
   Rnd 6: *K4, SKP; rep from * around.
   Rnd 7: *K3, SKP; rep from * around.
   Rnd 8: *K2, SKP; rep from * around.
   Rnd 9: *K1, SKP; rep from * around.
   Rnd 10: SKP all around.
• Break yarn and thread onto tapestry needle. Pull through all sts, tighten, and weave in end on inside.

Hat and muff are shown in Plush in colorway Cabin Fever, and in Fun Fur in solid Black, one size.

Brim

• Using 2 strands of B and size 9 straight needles, CO 12 sts. Work in St st until piece measures 19".
• BO all sts, leaving 6" tail for seaming. Sew tog end to end, taking care not to twist band.

Finishing

• Position fur band on outside of hat, along bottom edge. Stitch very loosely along both top and bottom edges of band to avoid making hat too small or inflexible.
• Weave in ends.

Muff Instructions

• Using larger needles and 2 strands of B, loosely CO 30 sts. Work in St st until piece measures 3".
• Change to 1 strand of A and work in St st for 9". (The Fun Fur will pull in slightly, but will stretch when muff is worn.)
• Change back to 2 strands of B and work in St st for another 3".
• Loosely BO all sts.

Finishing

Fold lengthwise and sew into a tube using mattress stitch or backstitch. Weave in ends.

Care

Hand wash both pieces. Hat will need to be shaped each time it is washed.

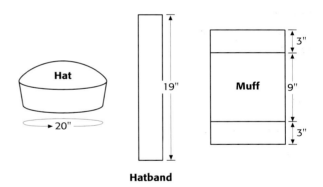

Ballerina Belle

By Lainie Hering

The idea of updating traditional Fair Isle knitting with hand-painted yarn has always appealed to me. Designer Lainie Hering agreed and liked the idea of introducing both the texture of a novelty yarn and the movement of hand-painted color into a classic design. She found that playful yarns easily lend themselves to clothing that will delight both little ones and their parents.

This updated Fair Isle cardigan is knit in one piece from the top down. Instead of making decreases to shape the neck and armholes, as you would when knitting from the bottom, you start with fewer stitches and make increases as you go. The raglan sleeves are generous by design, allowing freedom of movement and room for growth. Also, because the garment is worked from the top down, you can add length to both the sweater bottom and the sleeves as the child grows.

I selected a soft pima cotton called North Country Cotton, in heather-dyed cream and peach colors, for the body of the garment and a fancy novelty eyelash called Ballerina for completing the Fair Isle motif. It takes only a few touches of the Ballerina in the African Grey colorway to give this cotton cardigan designer appeal.

Vital Statistics

Skill Level: Intermediate
Children's Sizes: 4 (5, 6)
Finished Chest Measurements: 28 (29½, 31)"
Finished Lengths: 15½ (17, 18)"
Gauge: 5 sts = 1" in stockinette stitch on US 6 needles

Materials

All yarns are by Cherry Tree Hill.

Yarns:
Color A—3 (3, 4) of North Country Cotton (100% cotton; 4 oz/200 yds) in Peach Heather 〈3〉
Color B —1 (1, 2) skeins of North Country Cotton (100% cotton; 4 oz/200 yds) in Natural Heather 〈3〉
Color C—1 skein of Ballerina (novelty eyelash; 4 oz/200 yds) in colorway African Grey 〈3〉
Needles: US 6 and 5, 24" circular needles, or size needed to obtain gauge
Notions: Size F crochet hook; 6 star buttons, ⅝" diameter; stitch holders; stitch markers; tapestry needle

Stockinette Stitch

Knit all RS rows; purl all WS rows.

Cardigan Instructions

• With larger needles and B, CO 44 (46, 46) sts. Do not join.
• **Set-up row (RS):** K1, PM, K1 (seam st), PM, K8 (sleeve sts), PM, K1 (seam st), PM, K 22 (24, 24) (back sts), PM, K1 (seam st), PM, K8 (sleeve sts), PM, K1 (seam st), PM, K1.
• Turn, work 1 WS row, purling all sts and slipping markers as you come to them.

Neck Shaping

• Working back and forth, inc 8 sts on each RS row as foll: *Knit to marker, M1, sl marker, K1 (seam st), sl marker, M1; rep from * to end. Cont in this manner until there are 3 (3, 4) sts before first marker.
• Working back and forth, inc 10 sts on each RS row as foll: Inc 1 in first st, *knit to marker, M1, sl marker, K1 (seam st), sl marker, M1; rep from * to last st, inc 1 in last st. Cont in this manner until there are 13 (15, 16) sts before first marker.
• On next RS row, CO 5 sts. Do not inc in first

Cardigan is shown in size Small with main colors of Natural and Peach heathers, contrasted with Ballerina in colorway African Grey.

and last st. *Knit to marker, M1, sl marker, K1 (seam st), sl marker, M1 in next st; rep from * to end of row, CO 5 sts. St sequence on needles: front 19 (21, 22) sts; 1 seam st; sleeve 24 (26, 28) sts; 1 seam st; back 38 (42, 44) sts; 1 seam st; sleeve 24 (26, 28) sts; 1 seam st; front 19 (21, 22) sts. Total sts: 128 (140, 148).

Bodice Shaping

• Work number of rows in color listed by size:
Small and Medium: 4 rows C, 6 rows B, 2 rows C, 6 rows B, 4 rows C, 6 rows B, 2 rows C.
Large: 4 rows C, 6 rows B, 4 rows C, 6 rows B, 4 rows C, 6 rows B, 4 rows C.
• AT SAME TIME, to complete bodice, M1 on either side of each seam st (8 incs) EOR 6 (8, 9)

times, then every 4 rows 4 (2, 2) times. St count on front is now 29 (31, 33) sts
• Work even until striping patt is complete. Measuring along raglan-inc diagonal, sweater should be approx 7½ (7½, 8)". Sl all sts from each section on separate pieces of scrap yarn or st holders as foll:
Holder 1 (left front): 30 (32, 34) sts, which includes 1 seam st
Holder 2 (sleeve): 44 (46, 50) sts
Holder 3 (back): 60 (64, 68) sts, which includes 1 seam st from each side of back (2 seam sts total)
Holder 4 (sleeve): 44 (46, 50) sts
Holder 5 (right front): 30 (32, 34) sts, which includes 1 seam st
Total sts: 208 (220, 236).

Sleeves

• With larger circular needles and A, CO 5 sts, sl 44 (46, 50) sleeve sts from holder and work across row; then CO 5 sts. Total sts: 54 (56, 60).
• Dec 1 st on each end every 12 (13, 14) rows 4 times: 46 (48, 52) sts rem. Cont in St st until piece measures 10½ (12, 12½)". BO all sts.
• Rep for other sleeve.

Body

• Sl body sts onto larger circular needles as foll: With RS facing and A, work across front sts, PU 1 st along each of the 5 CO sts on each side of sleeve underarm (10 sts total). Join, and work across back sts, PU 1 along each of the 5 CO sts on each side of sleeve underarm (10 sts) total. Join and work across second front. Turn; 1 row complete: 140, 148, 156 sts.
• Work in rows until sweater measures 6¾ (7¼, 7¾)" from underarm. Change to C and work 2 rows. Work 6 rows in B and 2 rows in C. Attach A and work until piece measures 9 (9½, 10)" from underarm to bottom. BO all sts.

Finishing

• **Neck:** With RS facing and using smaller needles and A, PU 68 (70, 74) sts along neck edge. Work in garter st for ¾ (1, 1)". BO loosely.
• **Left front button band:** With RS facing, attach A to top of left front using crochet hook and sl st. Work 52 (54, 58) sc evenly spaced down to bottom of front, ch 1, turn. Next 4 rows: Sc in each st (including first st), working back and forth. Make sure you have 52 (54, 58) sts on each row. Break yarn and pull through loop to fasten off. Weave in ends.
• **Right front buttonhole band:** With RS facing, attach A to bottom of right front. Work as for left front for 2 rows.

   Row 3 (buttonhole row): Starting at bottom of front, sc in 4 (6, 9) sts, *ch 2 (this will form buttonhole), skip next 2 sc, sc in next 7 sts; rep from * 5 times; sc to top of neck, ch 1, turn.

Row 4: Sc to buttonhole ch sts, work 1 sc in each ch, making sure you insert hook under 2 loops of ch. Work in this manner to bottom of front.
Row 5: Sc in each st. Fasten off. Weave in ends on band.
• Sew underarm sleeve seams.
• Sew buttons to left front band to correspond with buttonholes on right front.

Care

Hand wash and lay flat to dry.

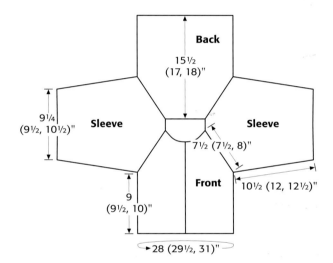

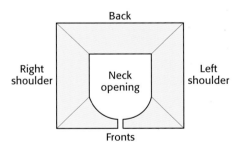

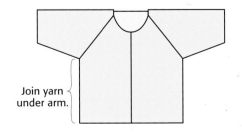

Dress Up, Dress Down

By Barbara Venishnick

This dress is knit in Gypsy Rose, a sunset colorway—one in which the colors advance toward a central shade and then retreat. With this type of yarn, striping can occur in small areas of horizontal knitting, so Barbara worked the skirt from side to side and created increases and decreases at the hemline to prevent striping or stacking of colors. For the bodice, stitches are picked up along the top of the skirt, where knitting from the bottom up moves the color in a new direction. For easier knitting and the best spread of color, wind the Ariel on a ball winder into a cushion that can be pulled from the inside and outside at the same time, or reserve about ¾ ounce and make a second ball. This will allow you to work the two back sections and both sides of the front neck at the same time.

Wide head and neck openings, as well as an open back with a small snap closure, avoid any fuss associated with putting a dress over the head of a small child. A little girl can simply step into the garment and let Mom snap the back. The flower pin is easy to knit one petal at a time, and it makes a great accessory that can be positioned anywhere on the garment.

Vital Statistics

Skill Level: Intermediate
Children's Sizes: 18 months (24 months, 2T, 3T, 4T)
Finished Chest Measurements: 20½ (21¼, 22¼, 23, 24)"
Finished Lengths: 18⅛ (18½, 19¼, 20, 20⅝)"
Gauge: 18 sts and 36 rows = 4" in garter stitch on US 5 needles

Materials

Yarn is by Cherry Tree Hill.

Yarns:
Color A—1 (1, 2, 2, 2) hanks of Ariel (65% cotton/35% rayon; 8 oz/515 yds) in colorway Gypsy Rose 🧶3
Color B—1 hank (all sizes) of Superwash Merino DK (100% washable merino wool; 4 oz/280 yds) in Slate 🧶3
Color C—1 hank (all sizes) of Superwash Merino DK (100% washable merino wool; 4 oz/280 yds) in Burgundy 🧶3
Needles: US 5 or size needed to obtain gauge
Notions: Size F crochet hook, 2 sets of snaps, pin back (optional), matching thread

Garter Stitch

Knit all rows.

Reverse Stockinette Stitch

Purl all RS rows; knit all WS rows.

Skirt

The skirt is knit from side to side, and then the waistband is picked up from the top edge.
• With A, CO 42 (44, 46, 48, 50) sts.
• **Rows 1, 3, 5, and 7 (RS inc rows):** Knit to within 2 sts of end, M1 (knit into front and back of next st), K1.
• **Rows 2, 4, 6, and 8 (WS inc rows):** K1, M1, knit to end.
• **Rows 9 and 10:** Knit even on 50 (52, 54, 56, 58) sts.
• **Rows 11, 13, 15, and 17 (RS dec rows):** Knit to last 3 sts, K2tog, K1.
• **Rows 12, 14, 16, and 18 (WS dec rows):** K1, SSK, knit to end: 42 (44, 46, 48, 50) sts rem.
• **Rep rows 1–18:** 14 (15, 16, 17, 18) more times.
• BO all sts loosely.

Dress is shown in fancy Ariel in colorway Gypsy Rose with Superwash Merino accent yarns in Slate and Burgundy, size 18 months. The removable flowers make this an easy garment to dress up or wear casually.

Waistband

With RS of skirt facing and using B, PU 92 (96, 100, 104, 108) sts along top edge of skirt (long edge that isn't scalloped). Work in rev St st for 9 rows.

Yoke

• With RS facing, change to A and work in garter st for 8 (10, 12, 14, 16) rows: 4 (5, 6, 7, 8) garter ridges.
• **Shape armholes:** With RS facing, K 20 (21, 22, 23, 24), BO 6 sts, K 40 (42, 44, 46, 48), BO 6 sts, K 20 (21, 22, 23, 24).
• Place first and last group of 20 (21, 22, 23, 24) sts on holders for back.

Front Yoke

• Working on center 40 (42, 44, 46, 48) sts only, knit 1 WS row.
• **Inc for shoulder caps:** On next RS row, K4, M1 (knit into front and back of next st), knit to within 5 sts of end, M1, K4.
• Knit 3 rows even. Cont to inc in same fashion every 4 rows 5 more times: 52 (54, 56, 58, 60) sts. Work 1 WS row even.
• **On next RS row, divide for neck shaping:** K 20 (21, 22, 23, 24), join second ball of yarn, BO 12 sts, K 20 (21, 22, 23 24). Working both shoulders at once, work 1 WS row even.
• **Next RS row:** K4, M1, knit to within 4 sts of neck opening, K2tog, K1. On other side of neck opening, K1, SSK, knit to within 4 sts of end, M1, K4.

- Work 1 WS row even. Cont to dec 1 st at each side of neck opening every RS row twice more; work even at shoulder edges.
- **Shape shoulders:** On next RS row, BO 4 (4, 4, 3, 4) sts, knit to within 3 sts of neck opening, K2tog, K1; on other side of neck, K1, SSK, knit to end.
- On WS, BO 4 (4, 4, 3, 4) sts, knit to end; knit to end on other side of neck opening.
- At beg of next 2 rows, BO 4 (4, 4, 4, 4) sts at shoulder.
- At beg of next 2 rows, BO 4 (4, 5, 4, 4) sts at shoulder.
- At beg of next 2 rows, BO 4 (5, 5, 4, 4) sts at shoulder.
- At beg of next 2 rows, BO 0 (0, 0, 4, 4) sts at shoulder.

Right and Left Back Yokes

- Place both sets of 20 (21, 22, 23, 24) back sts on needle and work at same time on separate balls of yarn.
- Work shoulder-cap shaping as for front, while keeping center-back edges even (no inc, dec, or neck shaping).
- When all shoulder shaping is complete, BO remaining 11 sts on each side.

Flower

The flower decoration is made in parts. A center section is made as one piece, and the outer petals are made individually.

Center Section

- With B, CO 6 sts. BO 3 sts, K3, turn.
- **Row 1:** K3, turn.
- **Row 2:** CO 3 sts, BO 3 sts, K3, turn.
- Rep these 2 rows 9 more times.
- BO rem 3 sts.
- Coil this "fringed tape" (think of rolling up a tape measure) tightly and sew by threading yarn tail on darning needle and poking it back and forth through 3-st base in various directions to keep roll stable.

Petals (Make 4)

- With C, CO 3 sts.
- **Row 1 (WS):** K1, P1, K1, turn.
- **Row 2:** K1, yo, K1, yo, K1.
- **Row 3:** K1, P3, K1.
- **Row 4:** K2, yo, K1, yo, K2.
- **Row 5:** K1, P5, K1.
- **Row 6:** K3, yo, K1, yo, K3.
- **Row 7:** K1, P7, K1.
- **Row 8:** K4, yo, K1, yo, K1.
- **Row 9:** K1, P9, K1.
- **Row 10:** K11.
- **Row 11:** K1, P9, K1.
- **Row 12:** K1, SSK, K1, sl2tog as if to K2tog, K1, p2sso, K1, K2tog, K1.
- **Row 13:** K1, P5, K1.
- **Row 14:** SSK, sl2tog as if to K2tog, K1, p2sso, K2tog.
- **Row 15:** K1, P1, K1.
- **Row 16:** Sl2tog as if to K2tog, K1, p2sso, pull yarn through last loop and weave in end on WS.
- Sew all 4 petals symmetrically around flower-center section at base.

Because this flower is knit one petal at a time, it is easy to imagine it having many more petals of unlimited colors.

Finishing

The best method for joining seams on this project is to use Ariel (color A) and a crochet hook to crochet the seams on the inside of the garment using slip stitch done loosely. Be sure to allow enough stretch in each seam as you crochet.

• Join front and back shoulders.

• Join CO edge to BO edge of skirt.

• Sew or crochet waistband tog at center back.

• **Neck edging:** With RS facing, use 1 strand of A and work a row of sc along bodice edges, starting at bottom of left back and working up back, around front neck opening, and down center right back.

• Weave in all ends. Sew a set of snaps at top of back neck. Sew a second set of snaps 1½" below first set.

• Sew flower to pin back, if desired, or directly to waistband.

Care

Wash this garment in machine, only if flower is removable, and do so on gentle cycle. Otherwise, wash by hand. Lay flat to dry.

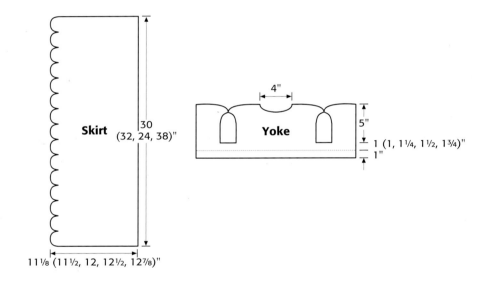

Knitting and Felting Accessories

FELTING adds another exciting possibility to the garment design process by dramatically changing the texture of the finished project. Felting knitted fabric shrinks it and changes the characteristics of the fabric. The felting process is made even more interesting with multicolor hand-painted yarns because the colors blend more as the yarn condenses. Felting turns yarn into actual fabric that is both wind- and water-resistant. Even the most basic animal-fiber yarns can give soft, furry results and produce fabric with more body and durability than plain knitting. Because much of the sizing happens during the felting process, it is also easy to hide mistakes, making felting a favorite finishing process for beginner knitters.

Common disadvantages stem from the fact that it is difficult to gauge what size to knit a project to achieve the desired finished size. Calculations are often necessary to achieve the correct proportions, and keeping a close eye on the washing machine as you're shrinking a project is a must. On occasion, a knitter may need to try felting several pieces before being satisfied with the results. This happens because once knitting is felted, it can't be undone or ripped out.

Felting is fun and the results can be fabulous, but doing it successfully depends on several variables: the washing machine, the water temperature, the water-hardness level (if your water is hard, it may take longer for an item to felt), and the experience of the person performing the felting.

The next five projects introduce knitters to easy-to-felt accessories that defy skill level. Basic felting instructions are given on page 108 with tips for achieving the desired results.

Five Felted Hats

By Diana Shannon

Living in the Northeast can be bone-chilling in winter if you are not properly dressed for what Mother Nature has in store for you. Diana Shannon designed these felted wool hats as the perfect way to ensure that your child stays snug, warm, and dry no matter how nasty the weather gets.

The colors of the hand-painted yarns fuse and flow into one another, creating a wonderfully soft look. But don't be fooled. Felted wool is virtually indestructible. It can also be re-wet and stretched a bit to allow for growth spurts.

Easy cast on, stockinette stitch, and simple decreases make these hats the perfect carry-along projects. The final felting process is a matter of tossing the garment into a hot-wash, cold-rinse cycle in the washing machine. Shaping the hat can be done simply by holding it and molding (pulling and patting) it with your hands. You can also place the hat over a bowl to dry. Diana gives all of her felted garments "haircuts" after they dry to trim the excess fuzz that forms during the felting process. You can also brush the surface with a natural bristle brush while trimming.

Vital Statistics

Skill Level: Intermediate
Children's Sizes: To fit toddlers; actual finished size depends upon felting
Gauge: 2.5 sts = approximately 1" in stockinette stitch before felting

Materials

Yarns are by Cherry Tree Hill.

Yarn: 1 hank of Lamb's Pride worsted paints (85% wool/ 15% mohair; 4 oz/190 yds) in color of choice (6)
Needles: US 15, 16" circular, for all hats; US 15, 24" or 29" circular, for hats 3 and 5; US 15 double-pointed needles (optional)
Notions: Stitch markers, pom-pom maker for hats 2 and 4, tapestry needle

Stockinette Stitch

Knit all rnds.

Hat 1: Basic Rolled Brim

• Loosely CO 72 sts. PM and join, taking care not to twist sts.

• Work in St st for 8½", ending at marker.
• Dec as foll, changing to dpn or 2 circular needles as necessary:
  Rnd 1: *K10, K2tog; rep from * around.
  Rnd 2 and all even-numbered rnds: Knit even.
  Rnd 3: *K 9, K2tog; rep from * around.
  Rnd 5: *K8, K2tog; rep from * around.
Cont dec as est until you complete rnd 13 (K4, K2tog). Stop working "knit even" rnds between dec rnds. Cont dec until last rnd: *K2tog; rep from * around: 6 sts rem.
• Work I-cord on these 6 sts for approximately 5" as foll: K6, then without turning needle, slide sts to other end of dpn or circular needles, wrap yarn around back of sts, and cont knitting. Rep this process until desired length is reached. Cut yarn, leaving 6" tail, and thread it through rem stitches; draw up tightly to fasten off.
• Weave in any loose ends.
• Felt hat, referring to instructions on page 108.
• Once felting is done, tie knot in I-cord. Trim knot end if desired.

Hat 2: Pinched Top

• Loosely CO 72 sts. PM and join, taking care not to twist sts.
• Work in St st for 10", ending at marker.

Basic Rolled Brim hat is shown in colorway Birches.

Pinched Top hat is shown in colorway Quarry Hill.

Ruffle Brim hat is shown in colorway Foxy Lady.

- Dec as foll:

    Dec rnd 1: *K10, K2tog; rep from * around. Knit 3 rnds even.

    Dec rnd 2: *K 9, K2tog; rep from * around. Knit 3 rnds even.

    Dec rnd 3: *K8, K2tog; rep from * around. Knit 1 rnd even.

- **Cont dec as foll:** Dec on each rnd (no "knit even" rnds in between). Each rnd you'll knit 1 less st between K2tog until there are no more knit sts between the K2tog: 6 sts rem.
- Cut yarn and thread through rem sts. Fasten off.
- Felt hat, referring to instructions on page 108. While still damp, make 4 equally spaced pinches on top of hat. When dry, tack pinches in place by taking 1 or 2 sts.
- Make pom-pom using pom-pom maker and referring to page 109 for instructions. Sew pom-pom to top of hat.

Hat 3: Ruffle Brim

- With longer circular needles, loosely CO 210 sts. PM and join, taking care not to twist sts. Knit 1 rnd even.
- **Rnd 2:** *K2tog; rep from * around.
- **Rnd 3:** Knit around. Change to shorter circular needles.
- **Rnd 4:** *K2tog, K1; rep from * around: 70 sts.

- Work even in St st for 8½", ending at marker. Total length from CO edge is approximately 9½".
- **Dec as foll:**

    Rnd 1: *K8, K2tog; rep from * around.

    Rnd 2 and all even-numbered rnds: Knit even.

    Rnd 3: *K7, K2tog; rep from * around.

    Rnd 5: *K6, K2tog; rep from * around.

    Cont as est until rnd 9: K4, K2tog. Stop working "knit even" rnds between dec rnds. Cont dec until you've worked *K2tog; rep from * around: 7 sts rem.

    Work last dec rnd: K2tog 3 times, K1: 4 sts rem.

- Work 4 sts in I-cord for approx 5" as foll: K4, then without turning needle, slide sts to other end of circular needles, wrap yarn around back of sts and cont knitting. Rep this process until desired length is reached.
- Cut yarn, leaving 6" tail. Thread it through rem sts to fasten off.
- Weave in any loose ends.
- Felt hat, referring to instructions on page 108.
- Once felting is done, tie knot in I-cord. Trim knot end if desired.

Pixie hat is shown in colorway African Grey.

Faceted hat is shown in colorway Tropical Storm.

Hat 4: Pixie

• Loosely CO 72 sts. PM and join, taking care not to twist sts.
• Work in St st for 8½", ending 2 sts before marker.
• **Next rnd:** K2tog, sl marker, K2tog, K32, K2tog, PM, K2tog: 68 sts rem.
• Knit 2 rnds even.
• **Dec rnd:** Dec 1 st on each side of each marker by working K2tog at each point: 4 sts dec.
• *Knit 2 rnds even. Rep dec rnd. Rep from * until 16 sts rem.
• **Next rnd:** *K2tog; rep from * around.
• Cut yarn and thread through rem 8 sts. Fasten off.
• Felt hat, referring to instructions on page 108; shape and fold point over to side while still damp. When dry, tack point to side of hat with yarn.
• Use pom-pom maker to make pom-pom. Sew it on with yarn.

Hat 5: Faceted

• With longer circular needles, loosely CO 120 sts. PM and join, taking care not to twist sts.
• **Rnd 1:** Knit even.
• **Rnd 2:** *K10, K2tog; rep from * around.
• **Rnd 3 and all odd-numbered rnds:** Purl.
• **Rnd 4:** *K9, K2tog; rep from * around.
• **Rnd 6:** *K8, K2tog; rep from * around.
• **Rnd 8:** *K7, K2tog; rep from * around.
• **Rnd 10:** *K6, K2tog; rep from * around: 70 sts rem.
• Change to shorter circular needles and work even in St st until hat measures 8" from CO, ending at marker.
• Dec as foll:
    Rnd 1: *K8, K2tog; rep from * around.
    Rnd 2 and all even-numbered rnds: Knit even.
    Rnd 3: *K7, K2tog; rep from * around.
    Rnd 5: *K6, K2tog; rep from * around.
    Cont dec as est until you complete rnd 9 (K4, K2tog). Stop working "knit even" rnds between dec rnds. Cont dec until there are no more knit sts between the K2tog: 7 sts rem.
    Last dec rnd: K2tog 3 times, K1: 4 sts rem.
• Either thread yarn through rem 4 sts and fasten off, or work 4 sts in I-cord (see page 108) for approximately 5".
• Weave in any loose ends.
• Felt hat, referring to instructions on page 108.
• Once felting is done, tie knot in I-cord. Trim knot end if desired.

Care

Hand wash all hats in cool water. Roll in towel to blot excess water. Shape and allow to air-dry.

A Family of Felted Mittens

By Donna Druchunas

These wintry mitts are perfect for playing in the snow or carrying books to school. The surface is water-resistant, while the interior is highly absorbent. In fact, wool can absorb as much as 30% of its weight in water without feeling wet to the touch. Mittens are small, quick, and fun to knit, and they leave a lot of room for creativity. Designer Donna Druchunas uses these small items as canvases for several different embellishments that can customize the mittens for boys and girls of any age. We chose all potluck wool yarns, using a hank from each color family: earth tones, watercolors, jewels, classic blues and greens, and brights, so you can see how just about any color combination will look when felted.

When knitting in the round, you need to join the cast-on stitches to form a circle without twisting them. If you can't tell if your stitches are twisted, work a few rows back and forth first. When you have about ½" of knitting, distribute the knitting onto three or four double-pointed needles and then join. You can use the cast-on yarn tail to sew the first ½" of the work together.

Vital Statistics

Skill Level: Intermediate
Children's Sizes: 4 (6, 8, 10)
Approximate Length before Felting:
7½ (9, 9½, 10)"
Approximate Length after Felting:
6½ (7½, 8, 9)"
Approximate Width before Felting:
3¼, (3½, 4, 4½)"
Approximate Width after Felting:
2¾ (3, 3½, 4)"
Gauge: 16 sts = approximately 4" in stockinette st before felting

Note: Exact gauge isn't critical, but make sure stitches are loose and airy for quicker felting. The felting process determines final size.

Materials

Yarns are by Cherry Tree Hill.

Yarn: 1 hank (per pair of mittens) of Potluck Worsted (100% wool; 4 oz/ 250 yds) in Potluck colorway of choice **④**
Needles: US 8 double-pointed, or size needed to obtain gauge, and US 6 double-pointed
Notions: Stitch holder, stitch markers, tapestry needle, size G or H crochet hook for optional embellishments, 18 g of 6/0 seed beads for optional beaded cuff

Garter Stitch (in the round)

Rnd 1 and all odd-numbered rnds: Knit.
Rnd 2 and all even-numbered rnds: Purl.

Stockinette Stitch (in the round)

Knit all rnds.

K2, P2 Ribbing

*K2, P2; rep from * to end of rnd.

Mitten Instructions

• With smaller needles, CO 24 (28, 32, 36) sts.
• Distribute sts evenly on 3 or 4 dpn. Join, being careful not to twist sts, and knit in the round, following instructions for desired cuff type.

Cuff

Work in St st for 1¾ (2¼, 2½, 3)", or choose one of decorative cuff options below:
Ribbed cuff: Work in K2, P2 ribbing for 1¾ (2¼, 2½, 3)".
Garter-stitch cuff: Work in garter st for 1¾ (2¼, 2½, 3)".
Beaded cuff: String half of seed beads on yarn. Work in St st for 1¾ (2¼, 2½, 3)", pushing bead

Basic mittens are worked with five different cuff options and embellishments for five totally different looks. Mix and match color families and cuff options to suit your family!

up to sts at random intervals every second or third rnd as desired. Beads will work themselves to WS of knitting. Turn cuff inside out so beads are on outside.

Beads add a great designer touch and are easy to add as you knit.

Thumb Gore

- For all styles, change to St st and larger needles.
- **Set-up rnd:** K1, PM, M1, K1, M1, PM, knit to end of rnd.
- Knit 2 rnds even.
- **Inc rnd:** Knit to first marker, M1, sl marker, M1, knit to second marker, M1, sl marker, M1, knit to end of rnd (2 sts inc).
- Cont inc every 3 rnds twice, then every second rnd 0 (0, 1, 2) time(s) until you have 7 (7, 9, 11) sts between markers.
- Knit even until piece measures 3½ (4½, 4¾, 5)".
- On next rnd, place thumb-gore sts (sts between markers) on holder and remove markers. CO 1 st over gap at thumb, join, and knit to end of rnd: 24 (28, 32, 36) sts.

Hand

- Work even until piece measures 5¾ (7¼, 8, 8½)".
- Decide if you want rounded or pointed tips on mittens and work accordingly, foll directions below.

Rounded Tip

- Arrange sts evenly on 3 needles as foll:
    - needle 1: 8 (9, 10, 12) sts;
    - needle 2: 8 (9, 11, 12) sts;
    - needle 3: 8 (10, 11, 12) sts.
- **Dec rnd:** On each needle, K2tog, knit to last 2 sts, K2tog.
- Knit 2 rnds even.
- Cont in this manner, dec every third rnd, until fewer than 10 sts rem. Break yarn, thread tail through rem sts, pull tight, and fasten off.

Pointed Tip

- Arrange sts on 3 needles as foll:
    - needle 1: 12 (14, 16, 18) sts;
    - needle 2: 6 (7, 8, 9) sts;
    - needle 3: 6 (7, 8, 9) sts.
- **Dec rnd:** SSK, knit to last 2 sts on needle 1, K2tog; SSK, knit to last 2 sts on needle 3, K2tog.
- Knit 1 rnd even.
- Cont in this manner, dec every other rnd, until fewer than 10 sts rem. Break yarn, thread tail through rem sts, pull tight, and fasten off.

Thumb

- Place thumb sts on 2 dpn. PU 3 sts from CO edge at top of thumb hole, using a third needle: 10 (10, 12, 14) sts.
- Knit even until thumb measures 5 (6¼, 7, 7½)" from CO edge.
- **Dec rnd:** K2tog around. Break yarn, thread tail through rem sts, pull tight, and fasten off.
- Weave in ends. Sew up small holes at base of thumb and at transition between beaded cuff and mitten (where you turned cuff inside out and worked in opposite direction).

Embellishments

Add crochet flowers, loops for attaching mittens to a jacket, or bows to any of the mittens if desired.

Crochet Flowers

Crochet these flowers and secure them to mittens before felting. The resulting flower mitten will look as if it were knit all in one piece.
- Ch 6, slip-stitch into first ch to join into ring.
- **Rnd 1:** Work 10 sc around ring.
- **Rnd 2:** *Ch 8, sl st into next sc; rep from * around entire ring.
- Break yarn and fasten off. Sew flower onto cuff of mitten or in desired location. Rep on second mitten.

Jacket Loops

As with the crochet flowers, knit the loops before felting and they'll become one with the mittens, making a sturdy loop for attaching the mittens to a child's jacket.
- With larger needles, start just below thumb and PU 1 st in each CO st on cuff of mitten. CO 8 sts at end of rnd.
- Purl 1 rnd.
- Bind off. Break yarn and fasten off. Rep on second mitten.

Knitted Cord

Knit I-cord and use to make a bow or mitten tie and attach them to the mittens before felting. Using dpn, CO 4 sts. *K4; do not turn. Slide sts to other end of dpn and rep from * until desired length. BO.

Bow

Work 4-st I-cord for 12". Tie in a bow and sew onto cuff of mitten or in desired location. Rep for other mitten.

Mitten Tie

Work 4-st I-cord for 30". Pull cord through knitting on cuffs of both mittens and tie an overhand knot to secure before felting.

Unfelted Ribbed Cuff

Unlike the other embellished mittens, these mittens are embellished with knit cuffs *after* felting.
• Using larger needles and with RS facing, PU 20 (24, 28, 32) sts on CO edge of mitten.

Tip: If you have trouble inserting a knitting needle or crochet hook through the felting to pull through the stitches, use a small awl or upholstery needle to puncture the felting.

• Work in K2, P2 ribbing for 1¾ (2¼, 2½, 3)" or desired length. Fold cuff to inside or outside of mitten as desired.
• Rep on second mitten.

Felting and Care

Put the mittens in a zippered pillowcase to catch the lint during felting (see page 108 for specific felting instructions). When the fibers are matted and you don't want the mittens to shrink any more, take them out and gently rinse them in the sink. Roll the mittens in a towel and squeeze out the excess water. Dry flat. Hand wash these mittens as needed. You might be tempted to toss them in the washer and dryer since they are already felted, but if they didn't shrink completely during felting, you might be surprised to see how much more the yarn can shrink.

Slipper Socks

By JoAnne Turcotte

JoAnne Turcotte loves the look of felted slippers, but as a knitting teacher, she feels that most slipper patterns are too involved for beginner knitters. Kids' feet grow so fast that she hates to spend too much time in the construction of a slipper. She wondered if a simple knitted sock, once felted, would yield a slipper-like result. She tried it and found that her simple slipper socks were a hit with both wearers and knitters, offering a practical alternative to more involved slippers.

These cozy slipper socks are easy to put on because there is no left or right. Cabin Fever and Northern Lights are warm neutral colors—great for either a girl or a boy. Their dark tones will hide any of the dirt that unavoidably gathers on the soles.

Unfelted, these slippers are just big socks, worked on a pair of 16" circular needles for most of the construction, rather than on double-pointed needles. A sock can easily be knitted in an evening. Plan on just two evenings to knit a pair and one evening to felt them.

Vital Statistics

Skill Level: Intermediate
Children's Sizes: Small (2–4), [Medium (5–7), Large (8–10)]
Finished Length of Foot: 6 (7, 8)"
Gauge before Felting: 10 sts = 4" in stockinette stitch

Materials

Yarn: 1 hank of New Zealand 14-ply wool (100% wool; 8 oz/270 yds) ⑥
Needles: US 13, 16" circular, or size needed to obtain gauge; US 13 (or 11) double-pointed
Notions: Stitch markers, stitch holder, safety pin, tapestry needle

Stockinette Stitch

In the round: Knit all rnds.
Back and forth: Knit all RS rows; purl all WS rows.

Slipper Socks Instructions

When slipping stitches, always slip as if to purl, except for the SSK. In that case, two stitches are slipped individually as if to knit, and then the two stitches are knit together to make a decrease.

Cuff

• Using circular needles, very loosely CO 32 (36, 40) sts. Do not join. Work back and forth in St st for 2 (2½, 3)", ending with RS row. Join, being careful not to twist sts. PM at beg of rnd.
• Work in St st until total length from beg is 4 (5, 5½)", ending at marker.

Heel

• K 24 (27, 30), then turn and work back (purl) 16 (18, 20). These are heel sts. (Leave rest of sts unworked on a holder.) Two heel rows have been worked.
• **Row 3:** Sl 1, K 15 (17, 19), turn.
• **Row 4:** Sl 1, P 15 (17, 19), turn.
• Rep these last 2 rows for total of 18 (20, 22) rows. Then work row 3 again for a total of 19 (21, 23) rows.

Heel Turn

Cont working on heel sts only.
• **Row 1:** Sl 1, P 9 (10, 11), P2tog, P1, turn.
• **Row 2:** Sl 1, K5, K2tog, K1, turn.
• **Row 3:** Sl 1, purl to 1 st before gap, P2tog (1 st from each side of gap), turn. (The "gap" is created when you turn the knitting.)
• **Row 4:** Sl 1, knit to 1 st before gap, K2tog (1 st from each side of gap), turn.
• Rep rows 3 and 4 until only 8 sts rem. Last row worked will be RS row.

The size Small slippers (left) are shown in colorway Northern Lights, and the size Medium slippers (right) are shown in colorway Cabin Fever.

Gusset

• Continuing with same needle, PU 10 (11, 12) sts from right edge of heel flap, PM (marker 1), K 16 (18, 20) sts from holder for instep, removing old beg of rnd marker when you reach it. Place new marker at end of instep sts (marker 2), PU 10 (11, 12) sts from left edge of heel flap, then cont to work across 4 sts from heel. Place safety pin to mark new beg of rnd. (If you use a st marker, it may be confused with the other st markers you are using.) Rem 4 heel sts will be first 4 sts of next rnd: 44 (48, 52) sts.

• Shape gusset as foll:

    Rnd 1: Knit rnd even.

    Rnd 2: Knit to 2 sts before marker 1, K2tog, sl marker, knit to marker 2, sl marker, SSK, complete rnd.

    Rep last 2 rnds until 32 (36, 40) sts rem.

Instep

• Knit rnds in St st until work measures 6 (7, 8)" from side of heel flap, then beg toe dec as foll:

Rnd 1: *Knit to 3 sts before marker 1, K2tog, K1, sl marker, K1, SSK*; rep from * to * with marker 2.

Rnd 2: Knit rnd even.

Rep these 2 rnds until 12 sts rem, changing to dpn when knitting is too short to do on circular needles.

Finishing

• Weave toe ends together using kitchener st (see page 108).

• Anchor yarn tail on inside and weave in all ends.

• Make a second sock, counting rows to make sure it is same size as first one.

• Felt both slippers at the same time in washing machine, referring to page 108 for instructions. Check often for size by trying slippers on child's foot. Shape during drying. Fold over top to create cuff.

Care

Hand wash and dry flat, reshaping socks as they dry.

Big Mouse Book Bag and Treasure Pouch

By Donna Druchunas

When Donna Druchunas was a lot smaller than she is today, her mother sewed her a mouse book bag. Somewhere along the way, Donna lost her bag, but she never forgot about it and has re-created it here in knitting. As a fun bonus project, Donna designed the smaller mouse bag to wear around the neck as a treasure bag or as an over-the-shoulder carrying case for a cell phone.

No kid will be able to resist a bag in the shape of a mouse! From Mickey, Mighty, and Mush Mouse in classic cartoons to the modern-day Itchy of the "Itchy and Scratchy Show" on the Simpsons, mice have always engaged the imaginations of the young and the young at heart. The neutral tones in this colorway are perfect for a camouflaged, natural-looking mouse. For a more playful look, try bright colors instead.

This bag is knit with a simple back-and-forth stockinette stitch. Single crochet is used for edging and the nose is embroidered. If you don't crochet, you can pick up and bind off knit stitches to create an edging. If you don't embroider, purchase a premade pom-pom or plastic nose from your local crafts store.

Vital Statistics

Skill Level: Intermediate
Sizes: Small treasure bag (Large book bag)
Approximate Finished Dimensions: 5¼" x 8½" (12" x 20") before felting , 4" x 5½" (11" x 15") after felting
Gauge:
16 sts = approximately 4" in stockinette stitch before felting on US 9 needles
12 sts = approximately 4" in stockinette stitch before felting on US 11 needles
Exact gauge is not critical, but make sure stitches are loose for easier felting.

Materials

Yarn is by Cherry Tree Hill.

Yarn: 1 (4) hanks of Potluck Bulky (100% wool; 4 oz/200 yds) in colorway of choice (**5**)
Needles: US 9 straight and double-pointed for small bag; US 11 straight and double-pointed for large bag
Notions: Stitch markers; crochet hook close to size of knitting needles you use; ½ yard of leather or suede cord for tail (small bag only); 1 skein each of black and metallic embroidery floss for nose and whiskers; 2 child-safe plastic eyes or sew-on eyes, ¼ (½)" diameter

Garter Stitch

Knit all rows.

Stockinette Stitch

Knit all RS rows; purl all WS rows.

Bag Instructions

The small treasure bag is worked with a single strand of yarn. The large book bag is worked with a double strand of yarn.

Back

- CO 13 (25) sts.
- Working in St st, inc 1 st at beg and end of each RS row 4 (6) times: 21 (37) sts.
- Work even in St st until piece measures 8½ (20)".
- Work 4 rows in garter st.

Head

- BO 3 (6) sts at beg of next 2 rows: 15 (25) sts rem.
- Work 2 rows even in St st.
- **Next row:** K 7 (12) sts, PM, knit to end of row.
- Purl 1 row.

If you are unsure about creating a large piece like the book bag, try the small bag first. It's quick to knit and felts easily.

- Beg dec as foll:
    __Dec row:__ Knit to last 2 sts before marker, K2tog, sl marker, K1, SSK, knit to end of row. Work 3 rows even in St st. Work dec row. Purl 1 row.
    Rep from * to * until 3 sts rem.
- Sl 1, K2tog, psso. Fasten off.

Front

Work as for back, up to instructions for head, and then BO all sts.

Ears

- PU 4 sts approx ½ (1)" from top outer edge of bag back where head begins.
- Working in St st, inc 1 st at beg and end of each RS row twice: 8 sts.
- Work 2 rows even. Then dec 1 st at beg and end of each RS row twice: 4 sts rem.
- BO all sts.
- Rep on other side of bag to make second ear.

Strap

If you prefer to make this into a backpack, follow the instructions for the strap on the Felted Backpack on page 106. To make the single strap as shown, use dpn, CO 3 sts, and work I-cord (see page 108) for 24 (36)". BO all sts.

Tail

• **For large bag:** Using a single strand of yarn, work 3-st I-cord for 15". BO all sts and tie a knot approx 1" from end of cord. Use a crochet hook to pull unknotted end of tail through center of bottom of bag. Tie a knot on inside to secure tail.

Finishing

• Sew front to back around side and bottom edges. Weave in ends.
• Work 1 row sc along diagonal edges of face.
• Work 1 row sc around each ear, skipping a st every now and then so crochet pulls in on ears, making them rounded.

Note: Every knitter crochets at a different gauge. You may have to redo the edging around the ears a few times until the ears curve to your liking. Crochet works up quickly and rips out even faster, so this won't add much time to your project.

• **Attach strap:** Fold bag at opening like a brown lunch bag, so it has inverted pleats at sides as shown. Insert strap as shown from back to front on each side, going through each part of pleats. There are no eyelet holes to weave strap through, but knitting sts should be loose enough before felting to insert knitted strap between them. Tie knot in each end to secure.

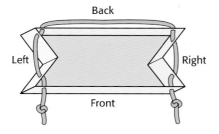

• Felt bag, referring to page 108 for general felting instructions.
• **Attach tail to small bag:** Use crochet hook to pull unknotted end of leather tail through center of bag bottom. Tie a knot on inside to secure tail.
• **Add nose and whiskers:** Cut 3 strands of metallic embroidery thread approx 6" long. With tapestry needle, attach strands to center of point on face. Tie strands in knot to secure and then separate plies. Using black embroidery thread, work vertical stitches for desired width of nose, then work horizontal stitches on top of vertical stitches, making stitches at top and bottom of nose slightly shorter to create rounded nose. Pull stitches very tight to create a dimensional effect.
• **Attach eyes:** Add purchased eyes, following manufacturer's instructions.

Care

Hand wash as needed. Dry flat.

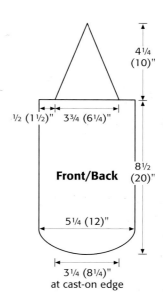

Felted Backpack
and Practice Purse

By Donna Druchunas

This bright backpack is perfect for carrying books to school or toys to a weekend at Grandma's. Because it's felted, it's practically kid-proof. It won't stretch out of shape from heavy or odd-shaped objects that might get stuffed inside. The smaller practice bag works perfectly as a little girl's purse or as a matching backpack for her favorite doll. Donna selected high-contrast jewel tones for these bags. If you want brilliant colors for the finished bag, pick a hand-painted combination brighter than you would normally choose.

There are a lot of steps to making this backpack, but none are complicated. Make the small bag first as practice for the techniques used in the backpack. Both bags are worked from the bottom up, with an optional pocket. The bag bottom is knit first, and then stitches are picked up around the perimeter of the bottom and joined to work in the round. The corners of the bag are marked with slipped stitches, and the center of the left and right sides are marked with a purl stitch. When the bag is finished and bound off, the fabric will naturally fold at the corners and sides.

Vital Statistics

Skill Level: Intermediate
Approximate Size before Felting: 8" x 10"
(13½" x 20")
Approximate Sizes after Felting: 6" x 7"
(12" x 14")
Gauge: 12 sts and 17 rows = 4" using 1 strand in stockinette stitch before felting on US 11 needles

Materials

Yarn is by Cherry Tree Hill.

Yarn: 1 six pack of Potluck Bulky (100% wool; 24 oz/1206 yds total) in colorway of choice ⑤
Needles: US 11, 24" circular, or size needed to obtain gauge; US 11 straight or double-pointed for optional pocket
Notions: Stitch markers; stitch holders; ½ yard of cotton cording, ½" to ¾" diameter

Garter Stitch (worked back and forth)

Knit all rows.

Stockinette Stitch

In the round: Knit all rnds.
Back and forth: Knit all RS rows; purl all WS rows.

Corner Stitch (CS)

To form corners, slip 1 st as if to knit.

Practice Bag Instructions

If you want to include the optional pocket on your bag, make it first so it is ready to insert when you reach that point of the project.

Pocket Lining (optional)

With straight needles, CO 16 sts. Work back and forth in St st until pocket lining measures 4", ending with WS row. Break yarn.

Bottom

• Using circular needles and a new ball of yarn, CO 24 sts.
• Work back and forth in garter st until piece measures 6". BO all sts.

Sides

• With RS facing, PU 80 sts around bottom as foll: 24 sts across front (CO edge of bottom), 16 sts along left side (left side of bottom), 24 sts across back (BO edge of bottom), 16 sts along right side (right side of bottom).
• Tie a strand of contrast yarn onto right front corner of bottom to mark beg of rnd. Join and work in rnds.

The small purse is a great project to practice on. Once you master it, knitting the backpack is a breeze.

• Set up fold lines as foll:
   Front: Sl 1, K23, PM.
   Left side: Sl 1, K7, PM, P1, K7, PM.
   Back: Sl 1, K23, PM.
   Right side: Sl 1, K7, PM, P1, K7.
• **Rnd 1:** Work in St st. When you reach corner marker, sl marker and knit corner st. When you reach side-center marker, sl marker and purl side-center st.
• **Rnd 2:** When you reach corner marker, sl marker and slip corner st (CS). When you reach side-center marker, sl marker and purl side-center st.
• Rep rnds 1 and 2 until sides measure 4" from picked-up sts.
• On next rnd of bag, make pocket opening (optional). Starting at beg of rnd, work across front as foll: Sl marker, work CS, K3, BO 16 sts for pocket opening, cont around bag, working all sts as est.

• **Insert pocket:** On next rnd, work all sts as est up to BO sts. Knit pocket sts in place of BO sts, complete rnd.
• Rep rnds 1 and 2 of bag sides until bag measures 2" from pocket opening.
• Work dec rnd as foll:
   Front: Sl marker (SM), CS, K2tog. Knit to 2 sts before marker, SSK.
   Left side: SM, CS, K7, SM, P1, K7.
   Back: SM, CS, K2tog. Knit to 2 sts before marker, SSK.
   Right side: SM, CS, K7, SM, P1, K7.
• Work dec rnd every third row twice more: 68 sts rem.
• Make eyelets for straps as foll:
   Front: SM, CS, K3, yo, K2tog, knit to 4 sts before marker, yo, K2tog, K2.
   Left side: SM, CS, K3, yo, K2tog, K2, SM, P1, K3, yo, K2tog, K2.

Back: SM, CS, K3, yo, K2tog, knit to 4 sts before marker, yo, K2tog, K2.

Right side: SM, CS, K3, yo, K2tog, K2, SM, P1, K3, yo, K2tog, K2.

• Work 4 rnds in garter st (knit rnds 1 and 3, purl rnds 2 and 4).

• BO all sts.

Finishing

• Sew pocket lining to inside of bag along sides and bottom. Weave in ends.

• Felt bag, referring to page 108 for basic felting instructions. To prevent eyelets from closing up during felting process, insert piece of ½"- or ¾"-diameter cotton cording through them before felting.

• Add drawstring strap to completed bag. You can use a twisted-cord, knitted I-cord, crocheted chain, or purchased cord.

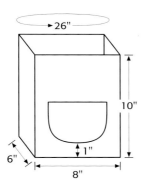

Backpack Instructions

The backpack has an optional front pocket with a flap. Make these two items first and set them aside until you reach the point on the backpack where they need to be inserted.

• **Pocket lining:** With straight needles, and single strand, CO 20 sts. Work back and forth in St st until pocket lining measures 8", ending with WS row. Place sts on holder. Break yarn.

• **Pocket flap:** With straight needles and single strand, CO 10 sts. Working in garter st, inc 1 st at beg of every row 10 times: 20 sts total. Work even until flap measures 2½", ending with WS row. Place sts on holder or leave on straight needles until needed.

Bottom

• Using circular needles and double strand of yarn, CO 40 sts.

• Work back and forth in garter stitch until piece measures 9". BO all sts.

Sides

• With a single strand of yarn and RS facing, PU 120 sts around bottom as foll: 40 sts across front (CO edge of bottom), 20 sts along left side (left side of bottom), 40 sts across back (BO edge of bottom), 20 sts along right side (right side of bottom).

• Tie strand of contrast yarn onto right front corner of bottom to mark beg of rnd. Join and work in rnds.

• Set up fold lines as foll:

Front: PM, sl 1, K39.

Left side: PM, sl 1, K9, PM, P1, K9.

Back: PM, sl 1, K39.

Right side: PM, sl 1, K9, PM, P1, K9.

• **Rnd 1:** Inc 4 sts each, evenly spaced on front and back, and 2 sts evenly spaced on each side on next rnd (132 sts).

• **Rnd 2:** Work in St st. When you reach corner marker, sl marker and knit corner st. When you reach side-center marker, sl marker and purl side-center st.

• **Rnd 3:** When you reach corner marker, sl marker and slip corner st (CS). When you reach side-center marker, sl marker and purl side-center st.

• Rep rnds 2 and 3 until sides measure 8" from picked-up sts.

• On next rnd, make pocket opening (optional). Starting at beg of rnd, work across front as foll: Sl marker, CS, K11, BO 20 sts for pocket opening, cont around bag, working all sts as est.

• **Insert pocket:** On next rnd, work all sts as est up to BO sts. Place pocket lining on 1 straight needle and pocket flap on other. Hold pocket lining behind pocket flap and K2tog across 20 pocket and 20 flap sts, knitting 1 st from pocket tog with 1 st from flap for each K2tog. Cont around bag, working rem sts as est.

- Rep rnds 2 and 3 for bag sides until sides measure 5½" from pocket opening.
- Work dec rnd as foll:
  Front: Sl marker (SM), CS, K2tog, knit to 2 sts before marker, SSK.
  Left side: SM, CS, K10, SM, P1, K10.
  Back: SM, CS, K2tog. Knit to 2 sts before marker, SSK.
  Right side: SM, CS, K10, SM, P1, K10.
- Work dec rnd every 4th rnd 3 more times.
- Make eyelets for drawstring closure as foll:
  Front: SM, CS, K4, yo, K2tog, knit to 5 sts before marker, yo, K2tog, K3.
  Left side: SM, CS, K4, yo, K2tog, K4, SM, P1, K5, yo, K2tog, K3.
  Back: SM, CS, K4, yo, K2tog, knit to 5 sts before marker, yo, K2tog, K3.
  Right side: SM, CS, K4, yo, K2tog, K4, SM, P1, K5, yo, K2tog, K3.
- Work 4 rnds in garter st (knit rnds 1 and 3; purl rnds 2 and 4).
- BO all sts.

Flap

- With a single strand of yarn and RS facing, PU 36 sts across back. Work in garter st for 9 rows.
- **Eyelet row:** K4, yo, K2tog, knit to last 5 sts, yo, K2tog, K3.
- Work even in garter st until flap measures 6".
- Dec 1 st at beg of every row 16 times (20 sts rem).
- BO all sts.

Straps (Make 2)

Using a double strand of yarn and straight needles, CO 8 sts. Work in garter st until strap measures 36". BO all sts.

Finishing

- Sew pocket lining to inside of bag along sides and bottom. Weave in ends.
- Felt bag, referring to page 108 for basic felting instructions. To prevent eyelets from closing up during felting process, insert piece of ½"- or ¾"-diameter cotton cording through them before felting. Also felt straps.

- Add drawstring to completed bag for easy closure. You can use twisted-cord, knitted I-cord, crocheted chain, or purchased cord.
- Attach felted straps to backpack with backstitch. Place straps side by side along the top edge of the back and stitch a 2" square at the end of each strap for sturdiness. Then stitch the bottom of the straps in place at the bottom outer edges of the bag back, stitching in the same manner. If the straps are too long for your child, they can be cut to desired length. The felted fabric won't ravel. Or, you can leave them long and just adjust them where they are attached to bag as your child grows.

Bag back

Care

Hand wash. Shape bag and allow to air-dry. This may take two or three days, so be patient. While felted fabric is fairly indestructible, your bag may shrink more if you machine wash or dry it.

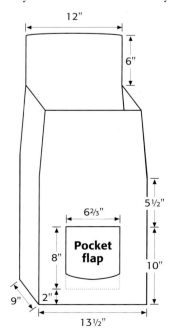

Knitting Basics, 1-2-3

In this section you'll find a compilation of techniques used throughout this book. The descriptions are by no means exhaustive, but you may find them handy as a quick reference guide. Use the short glossary that follows to familiarize yourself with new terms or to check abbreviations for stitches you may already know. In addition, you'll find yarn-weight and skill-level descriptions to help you select appropriate projects and substitute yarn as needed.

Buttonholes

In this book, buttonholes are made two different ways. In Very Cherry Vest on page 7, buttonholes are made by knitting two stitches together followed by a yarn over, which creates a hole but keeps the stitch count intact. On the next row, the yarn over is knit as a stitch, creating the top of the buttonhole.

In the pullover Garden Party on page 59, a single crochet chain is used to add a button loop to the finished edge of the sweater shoulder.

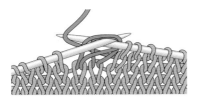

Knit 2 stitches together.

Yarn Over

Crochet

Crochet is often used in conjunction with knitting for making embellishments, adding buttonholes, and joining seams.

Chain Stitch: To begin, make a slip knot. Place the yarn over the hook and draw through the loop on hook to start the chain. Repeat for desired number of chain stitches.

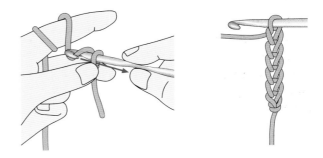

Single Crochet: Single crochet is often used to join seams. A crocheted seam tends to lay flat and adds little bulk to small garments knit for children. Another use for single crochet is to edge a garment or to join pieces that have been knit separately, such as flowers.

To single crochet (sc), begin with a chain stitch. Insert hook into previous knitted or crocheted stitch. Place the yarn over the hook and draw it through the stitch. You now have two loops on the hook. Place the yarn over the hook and draw yarn through booth loops on the hook. A single crochet stitch is complete.

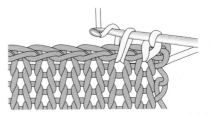

Insert hook into stitch, yarn over hook, pull loop through to front, yarn over hook. Pull loop through both loops on hook.

Felting

Place your garment or project in the washing machine along with two pairs of old jeans. (No towels!) To keep lint to a minimum, it's a good idea to put the project in a zippered pillowcase. Set machine on hot wash–cold rinse cycle, smallest load, and maximum agitation. Add a bit of detergent. (I've had good results with Arm & Hammer.)

*After washer has agitated for about 5 minutes, check the felting, remove garment and rinse in very cold water. This helps the felting process. Squeeze out excess water and return to the hot water in the washing machine. Repeat from *. Then let garment continue felting through rest of machine cycle, checking on it every 2 minutes until felting is complete. Some yarns will felt within the first few minutes while others may take two or three wash cycles. Allow to spin lightly to remove excess water. Remove garment and shape. Allow to air dry.

I-Cord

Knitted cord is often called I-cord, and it is made using double-pointed needles, although a pair of circular needles can also be used. This cording is handy for making decorative items such as the bows on the mittens on page 94, or purse straps or ties, such as those shown on page 98.

1. Using double-pointed needles, cast on 2, 3, or 4 sts, per the project directions.
2. Knit all sts, but do not turn work. Slide the stitches to the other end of the needle.
3. Repeat step 2 until cord is desired length; Bind off all sts.

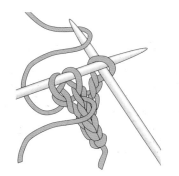

Increasing and Decreasing

Increases and decreases are used to shape a knitted project, such as armholes or necklines on a sweater.

Make 1 (M1): Insert the right needle under the bar of yarn between the last stitch knit and the next stitch to be knit. Lift the bar onto the left needle and knit into the back of stitch as if it were a regular stitch. One stitch has been made.

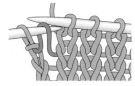
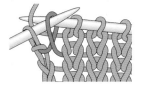

Insert left needle from front to back through "running thread." Knit into back of stitch.

Slip, Slip, Knit (SSK): This is a right-slanting decrease, used as a mirror-image decrease to the left-slanting K2tog decrease. Slip one stitch as if to knit, slip the next stitch as if to knit, place both stitches back on the left needle, and knit them together. One stitch decreased.

Slip two stitches to right needle. Knit two stitches together.

Kitchener Stitch

The kitchener stitch is used to join or graft live stitches from two different needles where a totally flat join is needed. This method is perfect for finishing the toes of socks, where a bulky seam would be uncomfortable.

1. You will need a length of yarn at least 1" for each stitch to be grafted. Thread it on a darning needle.
2. Arrange the stitches to be grafted on two needles, and hold the needles with the knitted work wrong sides together in your left hand.

You now have a front needle and a back needle. Attach the yarn to the back needle and work from right to left.

3. Bring the yarn into the first stitch on the front needle as if to knit, pull the stitch off the needle. Go into the second stitch on the front needle as if to purl, but leave the stitch on the needle.

4. Bring the yarn into the first stitch on the back needle as if to purl, pull the stitch off the needle. Bring the yarn into the second stitch on the back needle as if to knit, but leave the stitch on the needle.

5. Repeat steps 3 and 4 until all stitches have been woven together. Thread yarn through garment and anchor it on the inside, weaving in ends.

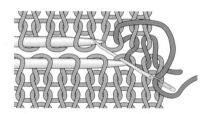

Pom-Poms

1. Use a purchased pom-pom maker, or make your own by cutting two cardboard circles to the size specified in your project. Cut a hole in the center of each circle, again referring to the project directions for the size. You'll have two cardboard doughnuts.

2. Thread a long piece of yarn onto a darning needle, and holding the two doughnuts together, wrap the yarn around the doughnuts as shown. Work evenly until the cardboard is completely covered. The more densely you cover the cardboard, the denser your pom-poms will be.

3. Cut a 12" length of yarn and set aside. Using sharp scissors, cut the yarn around the perimeter of the cardboard. Then, with the doughnuts still in place, run the 12" length of yarn between the two pieces of cardboard and tie the ends tightly to secure. Remove the cardboard and fluff the pompoms. Trim as necessary, and secure the finished pom-pom to your garment, following the project directions.

Three-Needle Bind Off (3-needle BO)

The three-needle bind off is used to join shoulder seams in one step, rather than binding off both the front and back stitches and then sewing them together. The result is a less bulky seam.

Place knitted pieces right sides together with needles parallel and pointing in the same direction. Knit two together (one stitch from front needle and one stitch from back needle). Repeat, and then pass the first stitch knit over the second stitch to bind off one stitch. Continue in the same manner until all stitches have been bound off.

Knit together one stitch from front needle and one stitch from back needle.

Bind off.

Abbreviations

beg	beginning
BO	bind off/bound off
CO	cast on
ch	chain stitch (crochet)
CS	corner stitch (slip 1 stitch at corner; used to shape bags knit in the round)
cont	continue
dec	decrease/decreases/decreasing
dpn	double-pointed needles
EOR	every other row
est	established
foll	follow/follows/following
g	gram
garter st	garter stitch
inc	increase/increases/increasing
K1tbl	knit 1 stitch through back loop
K	knit
K2tog	knit 2 stitches together—a decrease
kfb	knit in front and back of stitch—an increase
kw	knitwise
M1	make 1 stitch: knit a stitch on horizontal bar between last stitch worked and next stitch on left needle—an increase
m	meter(s)
mm	millimeter(s)
oz	ounce(s)
P	purl
patt	pattern
PM	place marker
P2tog	purl 2 stitches together—a decrease
psso	pass slipped stitch over next knitted stitch on right needle
p2sso	pass 2 slipped stitches over next knitted stitch on right needle
PU	pick up and knit
pw	purlwise
rem	remain/remaining
rep	repeat(s)
rev St st	reverse stockinette stitch
rnd(s)	round(s)
RS	right side
sc	single crochet
sl	slip
sl2tog	slip 2 stitches together
SM	slip marker
SKP	Slip 1 as if to knit, slip 1 as if to purl; then slip both stitches onto left needle and knit together—a decrease.
SSK	slip 1, slip 1, knit these 2 stitches together—a decrease
SSP	slip 1, slip 1, purl these 2 stitches together—a decrease
st(s)	stitch(es)
St st	stockinette stitch/stocking stitch
tbl	through back loop
tog	together
WS	wrong side
wyib	with yarn in back
wyif	with yarn in front
yds	yards
yo	yarn over

Standard Yarn Weight System

Categories of yarn, gauge ranges, and recommended needle sizes

Yarn weight	1	2	3	4	5	6
Types of yarns in category	Sock, fingering, baby	Sport, baby	DK, light worsted	Worsted, afghan, Aran	Chunky, craft, rug	Bulky, roving
Knit gauge range in 4" of St st	27–32 sts	23–26 sts	21–24 sts	16–20 sts	12–15 sts	6–11 sts
Recommended US needle size	1 to 3	3 to 5	5 to 7	7 to 9	9 to 11	11 and larger

Skill Levels

Beginner: Projects for first-time knitters using basic knit and purl stitches. Minimal shaping.

Easy: Projects using basic stitches, repetitive stitch patterns, simple color changes, and simple shaping and finishing.

Intermediate: Projects with a variety of stitches, such as basic cables and lace, simple intarsia, double-pointed needles and knitting in the round techniques, midlevel shaping, and finishing.

Metric Conversion

To easily convert yards to meters or vice versa so you can calculate how much yarn you'll need for your project, use these handy formulas.

Yards x .91 = meters
Meters x 1.09 = yards

Grams x .0352 = ounces
Ounces x 28.35 = grams

About the Project Designers

Donna Druchunas lives near the foothills of the Colorado Rocky Mountains, where she spends most of her time writing and knitting. Her designs and articles have been featured in *Family Circle Easy Knitting, Knitters, Interweave Knits*, and *INKnitters* magazines. Visit her on the Web at www.sheeptoshawl.com.

Lainie Hering works as a freelance pattern designer for Plymouth Yarn Company. Originally from New England, she resides in Florida in the winter and Maryland in the summer months. She has an Internet store, Cutie Pie Knits, which sells kits for baby sweaters and accessories.

Holly Rodriguez works full-time as a chemical lab technician. She has been knitting only two years, during which time she has designed and completed numerous afghans. Holly lives in Pennsylvania with her beautiful golden retriever, Noel.

Diana Shannon is a fiber artist recently retired from 31 years of teaching art in eastern Pennsylvania. With time to pursue her lifelong love of knitting, she now sells her unique felted pieces at juried shows and welcomes custom orders. She lives in Pennsylvania.

Terri Shea designs knitwear from her home in Seattle, Washington. She loves knitting for women and children and designs classic-styled patterns that are logical and easy to work.

Judy Sumner is a retired gerontologist, but knitters know her as a whimsical sock designer. Her patterns have appeared in numerous books and magazines. Here, she expands her repertoire to include children's wear, inspired by her twin granddaughters and the Smoky Mountains that surround her Tennessee Valley home.

JoAnne Turcotte works as a designer for Plymouth Yarn Company. She tests new yarns, designs garments, writes patterns, and serves as a technical editor on a variety of projects. In her "spare" time, she teaches knitting classes at Kraemer Yarns, a shop in Nazareth, Pennsylvania.

Barbara Venishnick is a nationally known designer and lives in northern Connecticut with her husband. She has been knitting since before she can remember and especially enjoys creating hand-knit garments from hand-painted yarns. Her designs have graced the covers of all the major knitting publications.

About the Author

CHERYL POTTER learned to knit at the age of eight. She knit her way through college and graduate school and was heavily influenced by Kaffe Fassett, whose book *Glorious Knits* inspired her first set of hand-dyed colorways. After earning her master of fine arts degree, Cheryl founded a hand-paint yarn company in 1994 called Cherry Tree Hill. In a milk house on her farm in Vermont, Cheryl dyed and designed wearable-art garments single-handedly until her yarns were "discovered" by *Interweave Knits* magazine in 1997. Cherry Tree Hill yarns are now sold in hundreds of stores throughout the United States and Canada, and Cheryl's work regularly appears in knitting magazines and catalogs. Today she is best known for her innovative and whimsically named colorways, painted on a variety of fibers both natural and synthetic.

During her years as a fiber artist, Cheryl has been a prolific writer and a teacher of classes that focus on fiber, color, and texture. She lives and dyes in a remote area of Vermont called the Northeast Kingdom. *Rainbow Knits* is her third book.